S. Hrg. 113–547

PROTECTING CONSUMERS FROM FALSE AND DECEPTIVE ADVERTISING OF WEIGHT-LOSS PRODUCTS

HEARING

BEFORE THE

SUBCOMMITTEE ON CONSUMER PROTECTION, PRODUCT SAFETY, AND INSURANCE

OF THE

COMMITTEE ON COMMERCE, SCIENCE, AND TRANSPORTATION UNITED STATES SENATE

ONE HUNDRED THIRTEENTH CONGRESS

SECOND SESSION

JUNE 17, 2014

Printed for the use of the Committee on Commerce, Science, and Transportation

U.S. GOVERNMENT PUBLISHING OFFICE

92–998 PDF   WASHINGTON : 2015

For sale by the Superintendent of Documents, U.S. Government Publishing Office
Internet: bookstore.gpo.gov   Phone: toll free (866) 512–1800; DC area (202) 512–1800
Fax: (202) 512–2104   Mail: Stop IDCC, Washington, DC 20402–0001

SENATE COMMITTEE ON COMMERCE, SCIENCE, AND TRANSPORTATION

ONE HUNDRED THIRTEENTH CONGRESS

SECOND SESSION

JOHN D. ROCKEFELLER IV, West Virginia, *Chairman*

BARBARA BOXER, California	JOHN THUNE, South Dakota, *Ranking*
BILL NELSON, Florida	ROGER F. WICKER, Mississippi
MARIA CANTWELL, Washington	ROY BLUNT, Missouri
MARK PRYOR, Arkansas	MARCO RUBIO, Florida
CLAIRE McCASKILL, Missouri	KELLY AYOTTE, New Hampshire
AMY KLOBUCHAR, Minnesota	DEAN HELLER, Nevada
MARK BEGICH, Alaska	DAN COATS, Indiana
RICHARD BLUMENTHAL, Connecticut	TIM SCOTT, South Carolina
BRIAN SCHATZ, Hawaii	TED CRUZ, Texas
ED MARKEY, Massachusetts	DEB FISCHER, Nebraska
CORY BOOKER, New Jersey	RON JOHNSON, Wisconsin
JOHN E. WALSH, Montana	

ELLEN L. DONESKI, *Staff Director*
JOHN WILLIAMS, *General Counsel*
DAVID SCHWIETERT, *Republican Staff Director*
NICK ROSSI, *Republican Deputy Staff Director*
REBECCA SEIDEL, *Republican General Counsel and Chief Investigator*

————

SUBCOMMITTEE ON CONSUMER PROTECTION, PRODUCT SAFETY,
AND INSURANCE

CLAIRE McCASKILL, Missouri, *Chairman*	DEAN HELLER, Nevada, *Ranking Member*
BARBARA BOXER, California	ROY BLUNT, Missouri
MARK PRYOR, Arkansas	KELLY AYOTTE, New Hampshire
AMY KLOBUCHAR, Minnesota	DAN COATS, Indiana
RICHARD BLUMENTHAL, Connecticut	TED CRUZ, Texas
BRIAN SCHATZ, Hawaii	DEB FISCHER, Nebraska
CORY BOOKER, New Jersey	

CONTENTS

PROTECTING CONSUMERS FROM FALSE AND DECEPTIVE ADVERTISING OF WEIGHT-LOSS PRODUCTS

TUESDAY, JUNE 17, 2014

U.S. SENATE,
SUBCOMMITTEE ON CONSUMER PROTECTION, PRODUCT
SAFETY, AND INSURANCE,
COMMITTEE ON COMMERCE, SCIENCE, AND TRANSPORTATION,
Washington, DC.

The Subcommittee met, pursuant to notice, at 9:35 a.m., in room SR–253, Russell Senate Office Building, Hon. Claire McCaskill, Chairman of the Subcommittee, presiding.

OPENING STATEMENT OF HON. CLAIRE McCASKILL, U.S. SENATOR FROM MISSOURI

Senator McCASKILL. This hearing will now come to order.

We have all heard and seen the ads promising quick and substantial weight loss if only you take this pill, drink this shake, use this device, or apply this cream—all without adjusting diet or increasing physical activity. It seems too good to be true, and, of course, it is.

We have a short clip of some of these ads—that have run on television, satellite radio, online, and in print—that I'm going to play so it is clear what we are talking about today. And it will appear in a moment.

[Video presentation.]

Senator McCASKILL. We also had a satellite radio ad I thought we were going to play—there are lots of terrible ads on satellite radio.

It's easy to understand why so many consumers are willing to take a chance, ignore their instincts, and believe suspicious claims like these. According to the most recent data from the Centers of Disease Control and Prevention, more than one-third of American adults are obese, and 70 percent are either obese or overweight.

This familiar story of the obesity epidemic is further colored by surveys finding a desire among Americans to lose weight, but consistently failing to put in the effort to do so. In 2013, a Gallup survey showed that 51 percent of adults wanted to lose weight, while just 25 percent said they were seriously working toward that goal.

This mismatch between Americans' stated desire to shed weight and their lack of serious effort can perhaps explain the growth of the U.S. weight-loss industry, as well as the proliferation of false and deceptive advertising for weight-loss products. With so many

(1)

Americans desperate for anything that might make it easier to lose weight, it's no wonder scam artists and fraudsters have turned to the $60-billion weight-loss market to make a quick buck.

Sadly, this is not a new problem. The Federal Trade Commission filed its first weight-loss case in 1927. McGowan's Reducine claimed in *True Romance* magazine that, quote, "Excess fat is literally dissolved away, leaving the figure slim and properly rounded, giving the lithe grace to the body every man and woman desires."

Since 1927, the FTC has filed more than 250 cases challenging false and unproven weight-loss claims, including, just this year, four settlements announced in January and, last month, a complaint filed in Federal court against the sellers of, in fact, a green coffee bean dietary supplement. More than one in ten fraud claims submitted to the FTC are, in fact, for weight-loss products.

But, the problem is much larger than any enforcement agency could possibly tackle on its own. Private stakeholders, companies that sell weight-loss products, media outlets, and other advertising platforms, as well as consumer watchdogs, must all do their part to help address this problem.

Media outlets and advertising platforms, in particular, serve as a critical gatekeeper that are well positioned to keep false and deceptive advertising from reaching consumers. I appreciate *TrustInAds.org,* which represents some of the largest online advertising platforms, being here today to discuss their recent report on this issue, the challenges online companies face in addressing false and deceptive advertising, and what more they can do.

But, the problem is not limited to the Internet. In preparing for this hearing, my staff reached out to a variety of media companies across all mediums to better understand industry practices in screening and monitoring advertising. I find it troubling that broadcast and satellite radio witnesses who were asked to be here today were unwilling to appear. To me, this indicates there is either something to hide or they don't have a good story to tell. Either way, we will not be effective in addressing this problem until all stakeholders take it seriously.

Like in virtually any other industry, there are good actors and bad actors. We will hear today from the Council for Responsible Nutrition, a trade association for the dietary supplement industry, and the Better Business Bureaus' Advertising Self-Regulatory Council about the industry's efforts to police itself.

We will also hear today from Dr. Mehmet Oz. He offers a unique perspective of being both a medical doctor and the host of a very popular daytime show that frequently airs segments on weight-loss issues and products, and that is frequently cited in the false-and-deceptive advertisements used to market questionable weight-loss products.

Dr. Oz, I will have some tough questions for you today about your role, intentional or not, in perpetuating these scams. When you feature a product on your show, it creates what has become known as "The Oz Effect," dramatically boosting sales and driving scam artists to pop up overnight, using false and deceptive ads to sell questionable products.

While I understand that your message is also focused on basics, like healthy eating and exercise, I'm concerned that you are melding medical advice, news, and entertainment in a way that harms consumers.

This subcommittee has looked at a number of scams affecting consumers. In most other cases, the scams resulted in financial losses, which can certainly be devastating. But, what makes weight-loss scams really stand out is that they not only result in financial losses, but can potentially put a consumer's health at risk.

I hope to hear suggestions today about how we can better empower consumers with the tools and knowledge needed to not fall victim to weight-loss scams and what more stakeholders can and should be doing to keep false and deceptive weight-loss ads from reaching consumers in the first place.

I look forward to hearing from all of our witnesses today, and I thank you all very much for being here.

Senator Heller.

STATEMENT OF HON. DEAN HELLER, U.S. SENATOR FROM NEVADA

Senator HELLER. Thank you. Thank you, Madam Chairman, for holding this hearing regarding the weight-loss industry.

I want to thank all our witnesses for taking time for being here also.

We all know that weight management is of interest to many Americans. I probably should add ''politicians'' to that, too. But, it's no surprise that the market is quite significant, totaling 60.5 billion in 2013, alone, in one estimate. I can understand the appeal these products have for many who are attempting to improve their health and lifestyles.

It seems to me, that many, and perhaps even most of these products and services are legitimate, making responsible, substantiated representation about health benefits and other claims. But, like any other marketplace, there are bad actors in this space who make widely erroneous claims about questionable products. There are also fraudsters and those who seize upon dieting fads and work to scam vulnerable members of our population.

I strongly believe the key to healthy weight loss is a combination of diet and exercise. I personally would be suspect of a magic weight-loss cure or a miracle pill. That being said, I can understand how a person may question their own assumptions when someone who they believe has credibility on the issue makes a claim about any particular product.

That's why I'm pleased we're here—joined today by Ms. Mary Engle, who is the Associate Director of the Division of Advertising Practices within the FTC Bureau of Consumer Protection. I applaud the FTC's work to shut down the scam artists, and I look forward to learning more about the Commission's success this year in bringing a series of cases under the agency's existing Section 5 authority against a number of companies engaged in deceptive advertising of weight-loss products.

I also look forward to hearing her thoughts about how the Commission is applying its ''reasonable basis'' standard for substantiating health claims, including weight loss, and what it considers to be competent and reliable scientific evidence to back certain claims.

While this standard has traditionally been a flexible one, it's no secret that the FTC has pursued more stringent requirements in recent consent decrees. It's an open question as to who these new substantiation requirements are meant to apply, where the FTC has followed its own procedural requirements in applying new standards, and whether the standard is consistent with constitutional protection of free speech.

I'd also like to welcome Dr. Oz here today. The Dr. Oz Show debuted in 2009, and reaches roughly 3 million viewers every day. I look forward to hearing from Dr. Oz on what steps he has taken to ensure that the information he shares, and conversation he moderates provides accurate claims.

We are informed that Dr. Oz does not endorse particular products, and he has been the subject of unscrupulous entities using his image in advertising without his permission. However, much has been written about the so-called "Dr. Oz effect," whereby demands for products and ingredients spike after they are featured on his show.

When the celebrity doctor mentioned "Neti Pots," for example, sales for the product rose by 12,000 percent and Internet searches for the device rose by 42,000 percent. It is this popularity that may have influenced a Florida-based company to enter the market in green coffee bean extraction, an ingredient that Dr. Oz referred to as a "magic weight-loss cure" and a "miracle pill" that can burn fat fast. This company is now the subject of an enforcement action brought by the FTC that is currently pending in Federal District Court in Florida for unfair and deceptive claims with regard to this product.

I would also like to welcome our other witnesses: Mr. Lee Peeler, for Better Business Bureau; Mr. Steven Mister, of the Council for Responsible Nutrition; Mr. Rob Haralson, of TrustInAds.org; and Dr. Daniel Fabricant, of the Natural Products Association. I thank all of you for taking time to be here today.

And thank you, again, Madam Chairman, for holding this hearing. I look forward to our testimonies and answers to some of our questions.

Senator MCCASKILL. Great.

Would you like to say a word?

STATEMENT OF HON. BILL NELSON,
U.S. SENATOR FROM FLORIDA

Senator NELSON. No, thank you.

Senator MCCASKILL. I think that my colleague just did a great job of introducing everyone, so I'll do this quickly. Ms. Mary Koelbel Engle is the Associate Director of Division of Advertising Practices, Bureau of Consumer Protection at the Federal Trade Commission, here in Washington. Dr. Mehmet Oz, Vice Chairman and Professor of Surgery, Columbia University College of Physicians and Surgeons, and host of The Dr. Oz Show. Mr. C. Lee. Peeler, President and CEO of Advertising Self-Regulatory Council, Executive Vice President, Council of Better Business Bureaus, from New York. Mr. Steven Mister—is it "Mister" or "Myster"?

Mr. MISTER. Mister.

Senator MCCASKILL. Mister. Mr. Steven Mister, President and CEO, Council for Responsible Nutrition, based here in Washington. Mr. Robert Hatton Haralson IV, Executive Director, TrustIn-Ads.org; and Dr. Daniel Fabricant, Executive Director and CEO, Natural Products Association.

And we will begin with your testimony. We will have you on a clock, which I'm sure you understand—I know you understand, Dr. Oz, about the clock—but, we are not strict about that. If you feel the need to go over by a few moments, we will not have a problem. And keep in mind, the entirety of any written testimony you would like to submit will be included in the official record.

Welcome, Ms. Engle.

STATEMENT OF MARY KOELBEL ENGLE, ASSOCIATE DIRECTOR, DIVISION OF ADVERTISING PRACTICES, BUREAU OF CONSUMER PROTECTION, FEDERAL TRADE COMMISSION

Ms. ENGLE. Good morning. Madam Chair and members of the Committee, I am Mary Engle, Associate Director for Advertising Practices at the Federal Trade Commission. I am pleased to have this opportunity to provide information regarding the FTC's efforts to combat fraudulent weight-loss advertising.

As you know, the United States is facing an obesity epidemic. Nearly 70 percent of U.S. adults are overweight or obese. Excess weight and obesity are major contributors to chronic diseases and healthcare costs, and present a serious public health challenge. So, it isn't surprising that there is strong interest in products that claim to promote weight loss. Unfortunately, where there is strong consumer interest, fraud often follows. In the FTC's 2011 Survey of Consumer Fraud, we found that more consumers were victims of fraudulent weight-loss products than of any of the other specific frauds that we surveyed.

Despite the continuing boom in the weight-loss industry, there exists very little scientific evidence that pills and supplements alone can help one lose a significant amount of weight. Scientists agree that the foundation of successful weight loss is to eat a healthful, calorie-controlled diet, and increase physical activity. Products that promote fast and easy weight loss without changes to diet or lifestyle deter consumers from making these tough but necessary changes.

As was mentioned, the Commission filed its first weight-loss case way back in 1927, and, since then, we have filed another 250 cases challenging false and unproven weight-loss claims. In the past 10 years, the Commission has brought 82 law enforcement actions challenging false or unsubstantiated claims about the effectiveness of a wide variety of weight-loss products and services. Since 2010 alone, the Commission has collected nearly $107 million in consumer restitution for deceptive weight-loss claims.

Our recent cases highlight how the agency has focused its enforcement priorities on large national advertising campaigns for a creative range of weight-loss products with unproven benefits. Operation Failed Resolution, announced right after the new year, targeted the newest weight-loss fads with popular ingredients: food additives, human hormones, skin creams, and acai berries. In one

Failed Resolution case, consumers were catchily urged to ''shake their Sensa'' and lose 30, 40, 90 pounds or more without dieting or exercise. In another, consumers were urged to rub in L'Occitane's almond shaping creams, touted as having body-slimming capacities that could trim inches in weeks. In a third, consumers with a taste for the rare might try liquid homeopathic HCG drops, made from a diluted form of human hormone, to lose a pound a day. Each of these cases resulted in a settlement with the FTC. The companies were ordered to pay consumer redress and to back any future weight-loss claims with well-conducted human clinical studies.

Despite this long history of FTC enforcement, weight-loss fraud persists. This is because it's an area where consumers are particularly vulnerable to fraud. There's an enormous amount of money to be made. And people intent on committing fraud will gravitate toward where the money is.

We have recently noted some disturbing developments with respect to weight-loss advertising. First is the reliance on proprietary studies using erroneous or even fabricated data. This was true in our case against Sensa and in our earlier case involving Skechers toning shoes. These kinds of practices add a layer of complexity to our weight-loss investigations.

A second trend is the appearance of weight-loss fads in mainstream media, supported by trusted spokespeople. Our pending case against NPB Advertising shows how the marketers of the Pure Green Coffee dietary supplement capitalized on Dr. Oz having featured green coffee bean extract on his show and calling it ''magic'' and ''a miracle.''

When consumers see products or ingredients marketed in sophisticated ways on respected media outlets or praised by hosts they trust, it can be difficult for them to listen to their internal voices telling them to beware. That is why we have long sought the partnership of the media to screen deceptive diet ads before they run. Our recently issued *Gut Check Reference Guide,* sent to media outlets throughout the country, advises the media on seven weight-loss claims that experts say simply cannot be true, and that the media should think twice about before running.

Finally, we recognize that consumers are the first line of defense against weight-loss fraud. The FTC has developed a full arsenal of consumer educational materials, ranging from traditional publications that lay out the facts for consumers to online teaser websites. And today we launched a new interactive online consumer quiz.

I want to thank the Committee for focusing attention on weight-loss scams and for giving the FTC an opportunity to describe its role. While we may never eliminate weight-loss fraud, we will continue our efforts to pursue the perpetrators, work with the media to help prevent fraudulent ads from running, and educate consumers that trusting their gut instinct can be a strong protective mechanism.

Thank you, and I'd be happy to respond to any questions.

[The prepared statement of Ms. Engle follows:]

PREPARED STATEMENT OF MARY KOELBEL ENGLE, ASSOCIATE DIRECTOR, DIVISION OF ADVERTISING PRACTICES, BUREAU OF CONSUMER PROTECTION, FEDERAL TRADE COMMISSION

I. Introduction

Madame Chair and members of the Committee, I am Mary Engle, Associate Director for Advertising Practices at the Federal Trade Commission ("FTC" or "Commission"). I am pleased to have this opportunity to provide information concerning the Commission's efforts to combat fraudulent and deceptive claims for weight-loss products.[1]

As has been reported for years, the United States is facing an obesity epidemic. More than one-third of U.S. adults (34.9 percent) are obese.[2] Combined with those who are overweight, the percentage skyrockets to nearly 70 percent.[3] Excess weight and obesity are major contributors to chronic diseases and present a serious public health challenge—the medical costs of obesity reached a staggering $147 billion in 2008, and the estimated annual medical costs of obese persons are nearly $1,500 higher than for those of normal weight.[4]

Last year, Americans were expected to spend $2.4 billion on weight-loss services,[5] and this figure is predicted to rise to $2.7 billion by 2018.[6] Where there is strong consumer interest, unfortunately fraud often follows. In our 2011 survey of consumer fraud, the FTC reported that more consumers were victims of fraudulent weight-loss products than of any of the other specific frauds covered by the survey.[7]

Scientists agree that the foundation of healthy, successful weight loss is to eat a healthful, calorie-controlled diet and to increase physical activity.[8] They also agree that even proven medications for weight loss should only be prescribed as an adjunct to lifestyle changes in order help certain patients adhere more consistently to a lower calorie diet.[9] Despite the continuing boom in the weight-loss industry, there exists very little scientific evidence that pills or supplements alone will cause sustained, meaningful weight loss. Moreover, the promise of fast or easy weight loss without changes to diet and lifestyle is especially pernicious because it may deter consumers from making the tough but necessary changes that are known to work.

Today I will provide an overview of the Commission's multi-faceted program aimed at combating fraud and deception in the weight-loss industry. I will first speak about the Commission's law enforcement program, then will explain our

---

[1] The written statement presents the views of the Federal Trade Commission. Oral testimony and responses to questions reflect my views and do not necessarily reflect the views of the Commission or any Commissioner.

[2] Cynthia Ogden, Margaret Carroll, "Prevalence of Childhood and Adult Obesity in the United States, 2011–2012," *Journal of American Medicine*, 311(8):806–814 (2014).

[3] "Weight Loss Services in the U.S. Industry Market Research Report from IBISWorld Has Been Updated," IBISWorld (Jan. 14, 2014), available at *http://www.prweb.com/releases/2014/01/prweb11486414.htm;* Cynthia Ogden, Margaret Carroll, "Prevalence of Overweight, Obesity, and Extreme Obesity Among Adults. United States, Trends 1960–1962 Through 2007–2008" (2010).

[4] Eric Finkelstein *et al.*, "Annual Medical Spending Attributable To Obesity: Payer-And Service-Specific Estimates," *Health Affairs*, 28, no. 5 (2009):w822-w831 (Jul. 27, 2009), available at *http://content.healthaffairs.org/content/28/5/w822.full.pdf+html.*

[5] "Weight Loss Services in the U.S. Industry Market Research Report From IBISWorld Has Been Updated," IBISWorld (July 22, 2013), available at *http://www.prweb.com/releases/2013/7/prweb10948232.htm.*

[6] *Id.*

[7] FED. TRADE COMM'N STAFF REPORT, CONSUMER FRAUD IN THE UNITED STATES, 2011: THE THIRD FTC SURVEY (2013), at 17, available at *http://www.ftc.gov/sites/default/files/documents/reports/consumer-fraud-united-states-2011-third-ftc-survey/130419fraudsurvey10.pdf.*

[8] *See* Mayo Clinic Staff, "Weight Loss: Strategies for Success (Make your weight-loss goals a reality. Follow these proven strategies)" (Feb. 26, 2014), available at *http://www.mayoclinic.org/healthy-living/weight-loss/in-depth/weight-loss/art-20047752* ("Hundreds of fad diets, weight-loss programs and outright scams promise quick and easy weight loss. However, the foundation of successful weight loss remains a healthy, calorie-controlled diet combined with exercise. For successful, long-term weight loss, you must make permanent changes in your lifestyle and health habits"); *see also* 2013 AHA/ACC/TOS Guideline for the Management of Overweight and Obesity in Adults: A Report of the American College of Cardiology/American Heart Association Task Force on Practice Guidelines and The Obesity Society (Nov. 12, 2013) (Accepted Article), at 20, Box 9, available at *http://onlinelibrary.wiley.com/doi/10.1002/oby.20660/pdf* ("Recommended methods for weight loss: Weight loss requires creating an energy deficit through caloric restriction, physical activity, or both. An energy deficit of ≥500 kcal/day typically may be achieved with dietary intake of 1,200 to 1,500 kcal/day for women and 1,500 to 1,800 kcal/day for men").

[9] *See* 2013 AHA/ACC/TOS Guideline for the Management of Overweight and Obesity in Adults, *supra* note 8, at 21, Boxes 10–12.

media outreach efforts, and finally, will talk about the importance of consumer education.

You might be surprised to learn that the Commission filed its first weight-loss case back in 1927; since then, we have filed hundreds of cases challenging false and unproven weight-loss claims. As the Commission staff stated in its 2002 Weight Loss Report, there exists "a never-ending quest for easy solutions." [10] The endless flood of unfounded claims being made in the weight-loss industry vividly illustrates the challenges we, and consumers, are up against.

Why, then, with such a long history of enforcement in this area, does weight-loss fraud persist? Unfortunately, there is no perfect answer. What we do know is that this is an area where consumers looking for a solution are particularly vulnerable to fraud; that there is an enormous amount of money to be made in the diet industry; and that people intent on committing fraud will gravitate toward where the money is.[11] While we might never eliminate weight-loss fraud, we will continue our efforts to pursue the perpetrators, to work with the media to help prevent fraudulent ads from airing, and to educate consumers on avoiding weight-loss scams.

II. The FTC's Weight-Loss Fraud Prevention Program

In the past ten years, the Commission has brought 82 law enforcement actions challenging false or unsubstantiated claims about the efficacy of a wide variety of weight-loss products and services. Since 2010 alone, the Commission has collected nearly $107 million in consumer restitution for deceptive weight-loss claims, and one weight-loss company paid a civil penalty of $3.7 million for violations of a prior Commission order.[12]

Our recent cases highlight how the agency has focused its enforcement priorities on large national advertising campaigns for a range of weight-loss products with unproven benefits. "Operation Failed Resolution," announced in January, targeted the newest weight-loss fads with popular ingredients—food additives, human hormones, skin creams, and acai berries.[13]

In our case against Sensa Products, consumers were catchily urged to "shake their Sensa" and lose 30, 40, 90 pounds or more without dieting or exercise.[14] We alleged that the defendants' powdered food additive, available in twelve flavors, was deceptively advertised to enhance food's smell and taste, making users feel full faster so they eat less and lose weight. Our consent order required Sensa to pay $26.5 million in redress; this money will be returned to consumers. The settlement also bars the defendants from making weight-loss claims about dietary supplements, foods, or drugs unless they have well-controlled human clinical studies supporting the claims, and it requires them to disclose any material connections with product endorsers or anyone participating in or conducting a study of such products.

The FTC's case against L'Occitane arose from that company's marketing of the Almond Beautiful Shape and Almond Shaping Delight creams, which it touted as having body slimming capabilities that could trim inches in weeks.[15] The Commission's settlement with L'Occitane bars the company from claiming that any product applied to the skin causes substantial weight or fat loss or a substantial reduction in body size, and also requires well-controlled human clinical studies for claims that drugs or cosmetics cause such results. L'Occitane paid $450,000 in consumer redress as part of its settlement with the FTC.

The Commission also filed a case against HCG Diet Direct in connection with its sale of liquid homeopathic drops, which contain a diluted form of hCG, a hormone produced by the human placenta.[16] Users were told they could lose up to one pound a day by placing the drops under their tongues before meals and adhering to a very low calorie diet. The Commission's consent order with HCG Diet Direct requires well-controlled human clinical studies; bars the defendants from representing that

---

[10] FED. TRADE COMM'N STAFF REPORT, WEIGHT–LOSS ADVERTISING: AN ANALYSIS OF CURRENT TRENDS (2002), available at *http://www.ftc.gov/news-events/press-releases/2002/09/ftc-releases-report-weight-loss-advertising.*

[11] See Frank Bruni, "Diet Lures and Diet Lies" *The New York Times* (May 26, 2014), available at *http://www.nytimes.com/2014/05/27/opinion/bruni-diet-lures-and-diet-lies.html?lr=0.* ("Enhanced education and growing sophistication haven't done away with fads. There's still too much favor to be curried and money to be made by trumpeting them.").

[12] *U.S. v. Jason Pharmaceuticals,* No. 12–1476 (D.D.C., filed Sept. 7, 2012).

[13] See Fed. Trade Comm'n Press Release, *Sensa and Three Other Marketers of Fad Weight-Loss Products Settle FTC Charges in Crackdown on Deceptive Advertising: Sensa to Pay $26.5 Million for Consumer Refunds* (Jan. 7, 2014), *http://www.ftc.gov/news-events/press-releases/2014/01/sensa-three-other-marketers-fad-weight-loss-products-settle-ftc.*

[14] *FTC v. Sensa Products LLC,* No. 14–cv–72 (N.D. Ill., filed Jan. 7, 2014).

[15] *L'Occitane, Inc.,* FTC Dkt. No. C–4445 (Mar. 27, 2014), available at *http://www.ftc.gov/system/files/documents/cases/140408loccitanedo.pdf.*

[16] *FTC v. HCG Diet Direct LLC,* No. 14–cv–00015–NVW (D. Ariz., filed Jan. 6, 2014).

a product is FDA-approved when it is not, and from failing to disclose any material connections endorsers might have to the defendants; and imposes a $3.2 million judgment.[17]

The Commission currently remains in active litigation against a number of other defendants hawking miracle weight-loss products.[18]

The Commission has noted several disturbing developments with respect to weight-loss advertising. First is the reliance on proprietary studies using erroneous or fabricated data. In response to our requests for scientific substantiation, companies usually will submit write-ups of human clinical studies, sometimes published in peer-reviewed journals. While these studies may appear facially plausible, in a number of cases, we have discovered serious flaws, or worse, outright fabrications once we obtain the underlying data.[19] In the Sensa case for example, the Commission alleged, among other irregularities, that Sensa's purportedly randomized control trial was not, in fact, randomized; that it included duplicate subjects; and that, on multiple occasions, the research firm Sensa hired sent results to the corporate defendants before the test subjects weighed-in. These flaws are not isolated to Sensa. In other cases, our examination of the underlying data has revealed altered, incomplete, or falsely-reported data.[20] It goes without saying that these kinds of practices add a layer of complexity to the FTC's weight-loss investigations.

Another distressing trend is marketers taking advantage of weight-loss fad ingredients that are propelled to popularity through exposure in mainstream media supported by trusted spokespeople. For instance, within weeks of an April 2012 *Dr. Oz Show* touting green coffee bean extract as a miracle fat burning pill that works for everyone, the marketers of the Pure Green Coffee dietary supplement took to the Internet making overblown claims—like "lose twenty pounds in four weeks" and "lose twenty pounds and two to four inches of belly fat in two to three months"— for their dietary supplement. The FTC investigated, and last month, filed suit.[21] The complaint alleges that the defendants deceptively promoted Pure Green Coffee through their website featuring footage from *The Dr. Oz Show,* supposed consumer endorsements, and purported clinical proof that dieters could lose weight rapidly without changing their diet or exercise regimens. We also allege that the defendants made deceptive claims on websites they set up to look like legitimate news sites and blogs, and on other "fake news" sites run by affiliate marketers whom they paid to advertise the Pure Green Coffee product. In all, the defendants are alleged to have sold more than 536,000 bottles of Pure Green Coffee since May 2012.

III. The Commission's Media Screening Guidance on Weight-Loss Claims

When consumers see products and ingredients marketed in sophisticated ways on respected media outlets and praised by people they trust, it can be difficult for them to listen to their internal voices telling them to beware. That is why we have long sought the partnership of the media to screen deceptive diet ads *before* they run. The FTC's recently-issued "Gut Check" reference guide advises media outlets on seven weight-loss claims that experts say simply cannot be true and that media outlets should think twice about running.[22] FTC staff sent this guidance document to

---

[17] The FTC's case against HCG Diet Direct followed on a set of warning letters the agency staff co-issued in 2011 with staff of the Food and Drug Administration ("FDA") to marketers of homeopathic hCG weight-loss products. The letters warned that the marketers were making unapproved new drug claims in violation of the Federal Food, Drug, and Cosmetic Act, and unsubstantiated claims in violation of the FTC Act. They also stated that the hCG products are misbranded prescription drugs. *See* sample warning letter from Mary K. Engle, Associate Director for Advertising Practices (FTC), and Ilisa B.G. Bernstein, Acting Director, Office of Compliance, Center for Drug Evaluation and Research (FDA) (Nov. 28, 2011), available at *http://www.ftc.gov/sites/default/files/documents/public\statements/joint-fda/ftc-warning-letter-concerning-product-labeling-human-chrorionic-gonadotropin-hcg-drugs/ucm281528.pdf.*

[18] *FTC* v. *HCG Platinum,* No. 13–cv–02215–HRH (D. Ariz., filed Oct. 30, 2013); *FTC* v. *LeanSpa LLC,* 3:11–cv–01715–JCH (D. Conn., filed Nov. 7, 2011).

[19] The staff's ability to obtain raw data may be hampered when such research has been conducted in a foreign jurisdiction.

[20] *See, e.g., FTC* v. *Skechers U.S.A.,* No. 1:12–cv–01214 (N.D. Ohio, filed May 16, 2012) (FTC complaint alleging that two of the four studies of the defendant's toning footwear were conducted by a chiropractor who was married to a senior vice president of marketing at Skechers; that one of the studies included spouses and parents of its co-authors as test subjects; and that some subjects who gained weight or increased their body fat percentage were reported as having lost weight or reduced their body fat percentage).

[21] *FTC* v. *NPB Advertising, Inc.,* No. 14–cv–01155–SDM–TGW (M.D. Fla., filed May 15, 2014).

[22] The Gut Check guidance identifies the following seven false claims for dietary supplements, herbal remedies, over-the-counter drugs, patches, creams, wraps, and similar products:

Continued

major publishers, media outlets, trade associations, and broadcasters asking them for their help in protecting consumers (and their own reputation for accuracy) by serving as a front-line defense, halting false claims before they are published or aired—and *before* consumers risk their money and perhaps even their health on a worthless product.[23] This is not the first time the FTC has issued such media advice,[24] and it likely will not be the last. Media response to our past initiatives has been positive and based on our experience, we expect that this effort will be successful in keeping many facially false weight-loss claims out of mainstream media.[25] As we have in the past,[26] we will follow up with media outlets (including television, print, and satellite radio) engaged in a pattern of running problematic weight-loss ads.

IV. Consumer Education Initiatives

The FTC seeks to educate consumers as well. The best protection against weight-loss fraud is a savvy consumer, so the Commission continually looks for new ways to reach consumers with messages about how to avoid falling victim to a diet scam. We have issued a number of consumer education brochures, articles, and blog posts that hammer home the message that the only thing consumers will lose is money if they fall for ads promising dramatic weight loss without diet or exercise.[27] The Commission also has created teaser websites designed to reach people who are surf-

---

(1) causes weight loss of two pounds or more a week for a month or more without dieting or exercise;

(2) causes substantial weight loss no matter what or how much the consumer eats;

(3) causes permanent weight loss even after the consumer stops using the product;

(4) blocks the absorption of fat or calories to enable consumers to lose substantial weight;

(5) safely enables consumers to lose more than three pounds per week for more than four weeks;

(6) causes substantial weight loss for all users; or

(7) causes substantial weight loss by wearing a product on the body or rubbing it into the skin.

The guidance is not intended to apply to prescription drugs, meal replacement products, low-calorie foods, surgery, hypnosis, special diets, or exercise equipment. *See Gut Check: A Reference Guide for Media on Spotting False Weight Loss Claims* (Jan. 7, 2014), available at *http://www.business.ftc.gov/documents/0492-gut-check-reference-guide-media-spotting-false-weight-loss-claims.*

[23] *See* model letter from Jessica Rich, Director, Bureau of Consumer Protection, to media outlets, available at *http://www.ftc.gov/sites/default/files/attachments/press-releases/ftc-has-up-dated-guidance-media-outlets-spotting-false-weight-loss-claims-advertising/140107gutcheckletter.pdf.*

[24] *See* Fed. Trade Comm'n, *Screening Advertisements: A Guide for The Media* (Dec. 2006), available at *http://www.business.ftc.gov/documents/bus36-screening-advertisements-guide-media;* Fed. Trade Comm'n, *Red Flag: Bogus Weight Loss Claims* (Dec. 9, 2003), available at *http://www.ftc.gov/news-events/press-releases/2003/12/ftc-releases-guidance-media-false-weight-loss-claims.*

[25] The Commission's earlier media screening initiative effort resulted in the number of obviously false weight-loss claims in television, radio, and print advertisements for dietary supplements, topical creams, and diet patches dropping from almost 50 percent in 2001 to 15 percent in 2004. *See* Fed. Trade Comm'n Press Release, *FTC Releases Result of Weight-Loss Advertising Survey* (Apr. 11, 2005), *http://www.ftc.gov/news-events/press-releases/2005/04/ftc-releases-re-sult-weight-loss-advertising-survey.* Recent monitoring suggests that this trend is continuing. It should be noted, however, that even though an advertisement does not contain an obviously false claim, it still may be deceptive for other reasons, such as for lack of substantiation for the core efficacy claim.

[26] *See* letter from Mary K. Engle, Associate Director for Advertising Practices (FTC), to Stacey Anne Mahoney (counsel for News America Marketing FSI, LLC) (Oct. 3, 2008), available at *http://www.ftc.gov/sites/default/files/documents/closing\letters/news-america-marketing-fsi-llc/081003newsamericaclosing.pdf;* letter from Mary K. Engle, Associate Director for Advertising Practices (FTC), to Nicholas R. Koberstein (counsel for Valassis Communications, Inc.) (Nov. 14, 2006), available at *http://www.ftc.gov/sites/default/files/documents/closing\letters/valassis-communications-inc./061114valassisclosingletter.pdf.*

[27] *See, e.g.,* "Putting the Squeeze on Bogus Weight Loss Products" (Jan. 7, 2014), available at *http://www.consumer.ftc.gov/blog/putting-squeeze-bogus-weight-loss-products;* "What's a Healthy Weight Loss Plan?" (Nov. 5, 2013), available at *http://www.consumer.ftc.gov/blog/whats-healthy-weight-loss-plan;* "New Year's Resolution: Don't Buy Into Diet Ads" (Jan. 8, 2013), available at *http://www.consumer.ftc.gov/blog/new-years-resolution-dont-buy-diet-ads;* "Weighing the Claims in Diet Ads" (Jul. 2012), available at *http://www.consumer.ftc.gov/articles/0061-weighing-claims-diet-ads;* "Weight Loss Promises: Health Information for Older People" (Oct. 2008), available at *http://www.consumer.ftc.gov/articles/0317-weight-loss-promises-health-infor-mation-older-people.*

ing online for weight-loss products.[28] And today, we are launching a new consumer quiz—the FTC Weight Loss Challenge—to help consumers identify weight-loss fraud. This interactive quiz is designed to help consumers think critically about weight-loss products and claims. Available in English and Spanish, the quiz separates fact from fiction in ads for products touting fast weight loss without the need for diet and exercise.[29]

V. Conclusion

I want to thank this Committee for focusing attention on weight-loss scams and for giving the Federal Trade Commission an opportunity to describe its role. The Commission is committed to continuing to use all the tools at its disposal to limit consumer injury from deceptive weight-loss advertising. I would be happy to respond to any questions about our weight-loss fraud prevention program.

Senator MCCASKILL. Thank you, Ms. Engle.
Dr. Oz.

STATEMENT OF DR. MEHMET C. OZ, VICE CHAIRMAN AND PROFESSOR OF SURGERY, COLUMBIA UNIVERSITY COLLEGE OF PHYSICIANS AND SURGEONS; HOST, THE DR. OZ SHOW

Dr. OZ. Thank you, members of the Committee, for convening this session—this hearing, and for allowing me to testify.

Consumer scams and fraud related to weight-loss products have plagued me in my work educating the public since I first started in the media, long before my talk show launched in 2009. It's a problem that I have spent immeasurable time, energy, broadcast resources, and money trying to combat. I'm chagrined to say the problem has only increased exponentially. However, I'm encouraged that the U.S. Senate has decided to prioritize this criminal enterprise, and I believe that the attention provided by this hearing and the contributions of other witnesses will help, because we can, together with our collective brainpower, douse the flames of this uncontrolled wildfire in the interest of protecting the consumer.

A bit of history. After I finished my training, in 1993—it was about a decade of training, by the way—I began practicing cardiothoracic surgery at New York Presbyterian Hospital at Columbia University. As I performed thousands of surgeries on patients whose hearts had been ravaged by obesity, I realized we needed to better educate people on how to take part in their own care. And, for that reason, I went into the public life in an effort to teach.

I started as a guest on the Oprah Winfrey Show in 2004 and had my first experiences with scam advertising at that time. When we discussed supplements like acai berry and resveratrol, there wasn't anything special about my description of them, but they—immediately, the Internet ads began springing up, using pictures of us, show quotes claiming that Ms. Winfrey and I were supporting these products and selling them. Ms. Winfrey and I and six attorneys general filed a civil suit against the companies making these ads. Despite the expense and law enforcement cooperation, it had very little impact. Ten years later, we're back. This phenomenon has grown dramatically in sophistication and scale so that I am forced to defend my reputation every single day.

---

[28] At first glance, the Commission's "FatFoe" teaser site appears to advertise a new product, "FatFoe," that falsely guarantees fast, easy weight loss for all users, with no diet or exercise necessary to lose up to 10 pounds per week permanently. *See http://www.wemarket4u.net/fatfoe/index.html.* However, when consumers try to order FatFoe, they learn the ad is a warning from the FTC about diet scams. *See http://www.wemarket4u.net/fatfoe/results.htm.*
[29] *See http://www.consumer.ftc.gov/sites/all/libraries/games/weightlosschallenge/.*

These ads take money from trusting viewers, many of whom believe that I'm actually selling the items. Just to be clear, in case it comes up, I have never sold supplements.

Out of sheer frustration, I have taken a number of measures to deal with this problem and protect my viewers. Recognizing—and I accept the responsibility for this—that the passionate language I used to describe supplements was fodder for these unethical advertisements, my show has tempered our editorial on promising supplements. We have been more stringent in presenting opportunities, and have included opposing voices on these segments. This, to my knowledge, has had no discernible impact. Marketers are still able to select a single phrase of support without the surrounding context, and continue profiting unimpeded.

The clip that you showed, and others of—similar ones—if you look deeper into the shows, I'll almost always mention something about the fact that there aren't crutches, they are designed for short-term support, you won't get there without diet and exercise.

To go further, I have devoted numerous shows to covering the exact anatomy of how a scam works and what to look for. I've launched a campaign called, "It's Not Me," and used various media partners to amplify the coverage. I devote a portion of every single broadcast to look directly into the camera—it's the last thing I say to the viewer—and tell them and reassure them that I don't sell anything. If they see my name, my picture, or any part of the show involved in an advertisement, do not buy the product. Check any show you happen to wander on, you'll see me saying that at the very end.

We also created *Oz Watch,* which is a way for viewers to report violations and report scams. *Oz Watch* has collected more than 35,000 complaints from our viewers. We even hired a private company to help with these complaints and police the Web, and have issued more than 600 cease and desist letters. After months of investigation paid for by us, I even confronted an egregious advertiser of Garcinia Cambogia on my show, in part because we found—this is the part that hurts me; Senator McCaskill, you mentioned this—not only was he using my—it's stealing my name—he was also only providing only 10 percent of the active ingredient. So, whether it works or not, that's a separate issue. If he doesn't have the product in it, it can't possibly do anything. By the way, last night, I went online. I was still able to purchase this product if I wanted to. It's a fairly shameless series of perpetrators that we're dealing with.

I have also taken action on my own, without the assistance of State and Federal agencies. But, I do believe that, working together, we can achieve a lot more.

Now, before offering any suggestions—and I have a few—let me address the criticism that my show may be fueling the Internet scamming problem. I'm respectful of these criticisms. I encourage a Nation searching for answers to their health woes. We often address weight loss, because, as you all mentioned, it affects about two-thirds of the population. If the only message I gave was to eat less and move more, which is the most important thing people need to do, we wouldn't be very effectively tackling this complex challenge, because viewers know these tips, and they still struggle.

So, we search for tools and crutches for short-term support so people can jumpstart their programs. We use the alternative solutions often—commonly used in other countries and other parts of the world, like in the Ayurveda tradition in subcontinent of India, traditional Chinese medicine. We feature cleanses and new diet programs by promising authors. Many of these are controversial, as are the supplements that we research and profile. But, I would rather have a conversation of this material on my stage than in back alleys, because the conversation will still happen, especially if you can give viewers the boost that motivates them to engage in wise dietary choices.

However, today is not a referendum on complementary and alternative medicine. We're not here to decide if vitamin supplements make sense. The problem we've been invited to discuss—Internet scamming and fraud—will begin to recede only when State and Federal agencies who have jurisdiction over the scammers amplify their enforcement and a public-private cooperative effort is undertaken in earnest that includes everyone on this panel in front of us, including the FTC, legitimate product manufactures, Internet ad-hosting services, and media outlets like mine. I need to be a part of this, I feel passionate about doing this, and I want to play a role.

Since my time is up, I'm not going to cover these suggestions, but I would like to offer some thoughts, maybe in the questions later on, about how we can create a Quick Reference Registry, Instant Device Whistleblowers, and maybe create a private-sector-funded bounty to assist the FTC in this very difficult, very challenging task.

Thank you.

[The prepared statement of Dr. Oz follows:]

PREPARED STATEMENT OF DR. MEHMET C. OZ, VICE CHAIRMAN AND PROFESSOR OF SURGERY, COLUMBIA UNIVERSITY COLLEGE OF PHYSICIANS AND SURGEONS; HOST, THE DR. OZ SHOW

Good Morning. Chairwoman McCaskill, Ranking Member Heller, Members of the Subcommittee. Thank you for inviting me to testify before the Committee today on this important issue. My name is Dr. Mehmet Oz and I am a cardiothoracic surgeon, Vice Chair and professor of Surgery at New York Presbyterian Hospital at Columbia University. I have authored or co authored over 400 published academic papers and studies. I have performed over 5,000 surgeries and was part of the transplant team at New York Presbyterian, performing heart and lung transplants in my early surgery career. I hold several patents on surgical devices related to valves and left ventricular assistance. I completed medical school at the University of Pennsylvania and also attended the Wharton School of Business.

I am also a public figure as host of the nationally syndicated Dr. Oz Show, author of YOU the Owner's Manual and the YOU Series of Books. I publish a magazine called Dr. Oz The Good Life with Hearst and I have a newspaper column which run in more than 110 newspapers across the country.

I am grateful for the opportunity to come before the Committee in the interest of protecting the consumer. The "consumer" to whom we refer is a person. That person is my viewer and your constituent. They have placed a trust in both of us for different reasons. You to represent them in the Senate and me to provide them with information that is useful, accurate and on which they make decisions. I would venture to say we both hold this trust to be sacred. But we are here because that "consumer" is now being preyed upon at an alarming and uncontrolled rate, and its incumbent on all of us here to work together towards a solution. I have laid out the testimony I plan to provide in the sections that follow.

Background

In the late 1990s and I was a surgeon at New York Presbyterian at Columbia in New York City. That morning I had performed a bypass on a woman who was 25 and obese. I had become accustomed to performing surgery on younger and younger patients who had advanced cardiovascular disease. There seemed to be more and more patients under the age of 30 whose obesity had caused life threatening disease.

The operation that morning was a success. I took solace in my usual post surgical reflection that I was a warrior in a medical field that had grown so adept at healing with steel and fixing hearts mechanically that there was little we could not do . I saw my department at New York Presbyterian Hospital at Columbia as the best in heart surgery and I could not have been more proud.

I went to check on my patient and although awake only a few hours, her family and she were celebrating with fast food—the very food that caused her heart disease. Then the thought struck me, No matter how many operations I performed, no matter how many hearts I fixed, nothing would really be impactful in reducing our Nation's number one killer unless people took responsibility for their part in prevention. Most of my patients could have avoided surgery by taking better care of themself. But most were completely oblivious to what role they played in whether they lived a long healthy life or succumbed to heart disease.

That evening as I reflected on the day, a conversation with my wife contained a breakthrough. I needed to reach more people my wife suggested—perhaps writing for magazines, authoring books and emphasized that she thought I might do well on television. Her suggestions were exciting, but I had no idea where to start and even less energy.

I knew I had to reach people before adolescence where they are most impressionable. I also knew that fitness and nutrition were not getting the emphasis they should be getting in our schools. Lisa and I formed Healthcorps after a successful pilot program in New York City and modeled it after the Peace Corps. But instead of developing countries, we work in high need high schools. We raise money to fund coordinators in high schools to teach mental resilience, fitness and nutrition and serve as full time instructors for two years. Since its start in 2003, Healthcorps has grown to over 60 schools in 13 states and the District of Columbia. We have impacted 300,000 students and nearly 600,000 members of their communities.

As the days and weeks went on Lisa's suggestions about television made more and more sense and we began to map out very practical steps. With a background in television production, she sketched out and produced a show that would explore topics in health and ignited interest by the Discovery Channel, who eventually decided to air our small startup talk show we called ''Second Opinion'' in 2003.

To launch ''Second Opinion'' we needed a big name guest and through a miracle of fate managed to book none other than Oprah Winfrey. Ms. Winfrey shared our concern that people needed to know more about their health and after her appearance on my show she invited me to appear on her talk show which was the number one talk show in the world. One appearance led to another and another and then a regular slot. Viewers were on fire with questions, e-mails, letters—all wanting to know what they could do to feel better, live longer, have more energy and most of all how to lose weight. We had hit a nerve. We had tapped into a collective thirst for information and inspiration about healthy living which really had no pop cultural thought leader. There were famous doctors, surgeons general, news correspondent M.D.s who were all excellent at their jobs. But while these predecessors did an fantastic job of reporting news, writing books and making policy, the public was looking for someone to also make health simple, fun, and less scary. We strategized that if we found a way add those elements, we might have a shot at engaging viewers enough to the point they change how they eat and live and move towards wellness rather than disease. The idea for The Dr. Oz Show was born in 2007 and development began.

History and Mission of The Dr. Oz Show

In fall 2009 we launched The Dr. Oz Show in the United States, it launched internationally in subsequent seasons and currently it is seen in 118 countries. The most succinct way to describe our mission was to make The Dr. Oz Show our national conversation on health. We wanted to provide information that viewers could act upon which would lead them to a healthy life. One thing I learned from Oprah Winfrey, television's greatest teacher, was that people didn't changed based on what they knew, they changed based on how they felt. This explained why my patients still smoked cigarettes despite knowing it would kill them. It was a huge breakthrough for me when I internalized that lesson, and the creation of the Dr. Oz Show aimed to translate that idea into a practical television format.

To make the Dr. Oz Show succeed in its mission, we have to overcome certain obstacles I learned in years of conversations with patients. We have to simplify complicated information. We have to make the material seem interesting and focus on the ''wow'' factor. We have to let the audience touch a liver, a heart, a brain, a spleen— things they would never get to do in their own lives. We need to have fun, use humor, and show people that laughter is a part of being healthy. It should be apparent to anyone who has seen our show that we are deliberately unorthodox in how we produce our program. We seek out the unexpected demonstrations, cos- tumes, dance routines. I have had various guests from circus performers to Surgeon Generals to real camels. I will go to any lengths to get people to think differently about health.

We also cover very serious topics. People need a filter for what they read in the news. They need interpretation that puts them at ease. They need information they can act on. They need to know how to care for loved ones. We cover cancer, diabetes, heart disease and all the major chronic diseases teaching basic prevention, how to be a smart patient, new and emerging research and alternative therapies. We see the show as the forum for a conversation on health that includes multiple points of view. While talk shows are designed to host debates, my medical training and each session of grand rounds at the hospital teaches that there are multiple ways to see a problem, and each point of view has its own value. Controversial issues like vaccines, mammograms, medical marijuana and many other topics are all part of our show. Viewer feedback is positive and our website has close to 4 million page visits per month.

Our website is the show's 24/7 informational concierge. I knew when we launched that we would never fit everything we need to in an hour, and people would have to learn about topics at their own pace. *www.doctoroz.com* provides both a solution and a platform. We are able to offer limitless content, show episodes, articles, blogs, lists and charts that people can print out and bring to their doctor, family history charts, recipes, exercise instructions—its where the viewer can go and get information.

By far, the topic that we are asked about the most is weight loss. We cover it frequently with good reason—its an absolute absolute pandemic in America and the largest driver of chronic disease. People feel powerless, they need solutions, they must lose weight to regain their health. We cover the topic from a physiological, nutritional and emotional angle—from calories to body image and supplements to plastic surgery. These conversations are already taking place everywhere in in our country as people grapple with the Nation's weight problem. We are one of the very few—possibly sole media outlets whose mission includes dedication to the issue.

Editorial Coverage of Vitamins and Supplements

It is estimated that 150 million Americans—roughly 2/3—take vitamins and supplements. Plain and simple these products alter body chemistry—ideally in a positive way. Up until we launched, there was no designated thought leader that deciphered the bottom line for consumers on what supplements were helpful and why. With nutritional supplements top of mind for our audience and the great risks and rewards that result form their consumption, we actively research new and emerging products and trends and news about products found in the average health food store. We look to published research, expert guests, our own testing that we do with third party laboratories and anecdotal testimony from audience members about people's experience with the various products with the goal of providing useful information. Our audience is already targeted by manufacturers and they need better information.

We have aired close to 900 shows in the five seasons since we launched, and while we cover the entire range of health topics, the vitamins and supplements, especially those for weight loss have generated a disproportionate amount of attention. Most of the time, the general public is hearing about a product on my show for the first time and there is genuine curiosity. Other times the market springs into action, often illicitly and a surge of ads appear every time you turn on a computer.

The general media covers a lot of what we do on the show in various ways, and I appear regularly on other programs to discuss news or other topics. More than once there has been criticism from some reporters who took exception to my use of colorful language in the supplement segments. They have expressed disagreement with my use of words like ''miracle'' and ''groundbreaking''. We constantly reflect as a show on which words are the right ones to use and which adjectives we may want to retire. We are always self correcting, progressing, trying to make a better show. Do we miss the mark sometimes? Of course. But our work is affirmed by the millions of e-mails, testimonials, phone calls, from people who say they saw something on our show that made a difference in their lives and they are better off. Its affirmed by the 1.5 million people who signed up for season long Transformation Nation Program in Season 3 and lost 3 Million pounds through healthier behavior they learned from watching. Its affirmed by the two million people who downloaded our New Year's diet plan this January and the 500,000 that printed out the family history chart to fill out and bring to their doctor. These are just a few examples, but they confirm for us that we are speaking in a language that resonates with our audience.

In 2012, we aired a show on a little known supplement called Green Coffee Extract. This is the supplement that is so prevalent in all the ads that are being exhibited today.

In this show I used the word ''miracle'' when referring to how green coffee could melt fat and I explored a new study on the supplement. I was enthusiastic that it could be a tool to assist people in losing weight and I knew the audience wanted and needed this information. After the show aired an explosion of ads and marketing followed along with criticism that our characterization went to far in describing green coffee. My way of dealing with it was to construct a second show and answer the criticism of our original segment. While we covered Green Coffee in the show, we devoted about half of the hour to me explaining to viewers that they are being duped by unscrupulous people who are illegally using my name in ads. The entire discussion of Green Coffee was prefaced with a warning to the viewer in the interest of protecting them.

Most importantly, in this show I spent an enormous portion of the broadcast demonstrating the false ads and how the various retail scams work—again trying to protect the viewer. I also re-explored green coffee this time using the audience to reveal their anecdotal experience after trying the supplement for two weeks. Some had lost weight, others had not. It seemed to help some people in their weight loss efforts. The Internet lit up again, the illicit ads proliferated, and we faced additional criticism.

Because of the cause and effect that green coffee show had on the now burgeoning scams which were increasing completely unchecked, we took a long hard look at how we could minimize that effect and where our editorial could play a role, while simultaneously devising measures to protect the viewer and giving them a mechanism to report scams. After constantly reflecting on and refining our language, we broadcast a show in February 2014, two seasons later on a little known food called Yacon syrup, which is a sweetener made from a South American root vegetable and has been in stores for decades. We were deliberately measured in our language. We didn't use the words ''miracle'' or ''magic,'' we thoroughly listed the potential side effects such as it cause diarrhea in some of our audience members who tried it. But I did suggest that it was good alternative sweetener and could assist in weight loss efforts. But the same thing happened afterwards—the very next day Yacon syrup was the subject of countless ads, many with my name and face with the exact same motus operandi as every ad on every supplement that had come before it. This taught me that regardless of how much enthusiasm I show in a segment, and whether I use forceful words like ''miracle,'' and ''magic'' or more conservative language like ''breakthrough,'' or ''promising'' the result is the same—my viewers are still victims of fraud and false claims by a sophisticated, large scale organized criminal enterprise that is being allowed to operate fully and without any enforcement effort. This concerned me greatly.

Now completely confounded by this rampant problem, my next solution was to develop a show in which we found one of these perpetrators and confronted them. I thought if I made an example out of a company that was hard at work deceiving viewers that I would be protecting my audience and scaring others doing the same. We aired a show on May 2014 where I staked out and confronted a company in San Diego that was selling Garcinia Cambogia under the name ''Miracle Garcinia''. Sadly, this had little impact on the proliferation of the ad scams as well.

So I stand before you today as a someone who has done everything possible to try to protect my audience against those who attempt to hijack the conversation between viewer and doctor. I have collected close to 35,000 complaints, each one representing a real person—your constituents—who have been the victim of some type of fraud.

When we write a script, we need to generate enthusiasm and engage the viewer. Viewers do not watch our show because they are seeking our dry clinical language. Viewers watch because we use language that is familiar to them which they would use when speaking to friends and loved ones. We are a guest in their home every afternoon. To treat that privilege like an academic lecture in medical school would be a miscalculation. As a television show, unlike a scientific conference, we have both the luxury and necessity to use colloquialisms and vernacular that you probably won't hear at your doctor's office. This is the essence of why we break through to viewer—we meet them where they are instead of demand they traverse a river of dry, confusing terms that are sure to alienate them. Remember—people act on emotion and how they feel, so a main principle in building our scripts is to illicit a visceral, emotional reaction from the viewer.

Trademark Infringement and Illicit Advertising of Products Involving the Dr. Oz Show

Let me be very clear on the following: *I do not endorse any products or receive any money from any products that are sold. I have never allowed my image to be used in any ad. If you see my name, face or show in any type of ad, e-mail or other circumstance, its illegal.*

I have been grappling with the problem of illicit use of my name connected to weight-loss scams and other products since before The Dr. Oz Show even launched. In the years that I was a regular guest on The Oprah Winfrey Show, I covered two products—Acai Berry and Resveratrol, which lead to a tsunami of illegal banner ads on the internet. That began my long battle with this complicated and insidious problem. Below is a timeline and explanations on the effort the Dr. Oz Show has undertaken since that time.

9/12/2009: Dr. Oz and Oprah Winfrey *file civil suit* against merchants using their likeness to sell and promote acai berry.

Working with attorneys general form six states combined with our civil suit, we shut down 40 companies that were responsible for the false advertising. The effort received enormous news coverage. Sadly, after many were shut down, an equal amount re-appeared soon after and within a year the amount of perpetrators had more then tripled. In the five years since that lawsuit the amount of businesses responsible for the illicit scams is without measure.

9/03/2012: Dr. Oz Announces *Oz Watch* "If you see something, send something"

Stymied by the uncontrolled proliferation of Internet scams involving our stoled trademark, we created a web based reporting system for viewers to turn in a URL, spam e-mail, commercial, or any use of my likeness or of the show. We told the audience to share anything they find while reminding them never to purchase a product that uses my likeness or the show. Since its launch in 2012, we have collected 35,000 complaints. Many of the reports are viewers who are the victims of overt crimes and have had their credit cards billed repeatedly despite efforts to discontinue purchasing. These complaints are available to the Committee today and to any state or Federal agency that wishes to review them in order to take action.

9/12/2012: *"Dr. Oz Fights to Reclaim His Name"* Show

We devoted a show to explaining to the viewer the exact nature of how these scams work and how easy it is for the companies to operate. We used this broadcast time which otherwise would have been spent on useful health editorial content teaching the audience how to navigate what had become a treacherous environment as the illicit ads and scams continued to increase.

5/06/2013: Dr. Oz Announces the *"It's Not Me"* Campaign

With the illicit ads and scams now at fever pitch and growing exponentially, we launched a very public campaign with various media outlets to remind the public not to buy any products using my likeness. The campaign devoted a portion of each broadcast to remind viewers that I sell no products and have no relationship with any vitamin, supplement or weight loss manufacturers and to NEVER buy anything they see using my name. That campaign is still underway and will continue in perpetuity as a consumer protection measure.

4/29/2014: *"Dr. Oz Takes Down the Scammers"* Show

Using the power of the show platform, and frustrated by the scale of the problem we developed a show that investigated, staked out and finally confronted a company that was an egregious example of the Internet scams. This dramatic show can be reviewed on *www.doctoroz.com* and was an attempt to send a message to compaies that if they choose to skirt the law, we will find them and we will expose them.

The breakdown of content collected in the Ozwatch effort is as follows:

Total Cases Reported to Oz Watch through 5/31/2014: 35,000+

• *"High Value" Targets (image/logo/video infringements) identified: 9,000+*

Many reported offenses (thousands) are duplicates. This number excludes social media.

- *C&Ds sent to date: 600 (not including YouTube and Facebook takedowns) to 450+ sites.*

Sites taken down + Infringements removed in response to C&D: 300+

C&Ds sent that produced no result: 78

Average Claims Submitted to Oz Watch Per Day: 50

Total YouTube Takedowns to Date: 4,700+ videos

Total SPAM Messages Reported: 28,000+

General breakdown by claim type (not exact):

- *Online: Website, Facebook, Amazon: 62 percent*
- *E-mail/Text: 28 percent*
- *Other (Television/Radio/Print): 9 percent*
- *In-store: 1 percent*

Analysis of a Scam

The following are the types of scams and the mechanisms that we have identified:

ONLINE DIRECT MARKETING

Online direct marketers design and leverage unscrupulous business tactics that are intended to elicit an immediate response or action from prospective consumers.

To reach potential buyers, direct marketers employ a variety of proven tactics including: display/banner advertisements, targeted ad words (via Google/Facebook, etc), direct marketing via e-mail and text message and traditional broadcast media. Each method typically features an unauthorized image or video of a celebrity and a number of trusted consumer facing brands that are intended to establish a sense of trust and familiarity in the prospective buyer.

ADVERTORIALS + FREE TRIALS

The celebrity images and trusted brands are presented alongside consumer and celebrity "testimonials" on pages that are considered "Advertorial". They display celebrity images and selectively edit trademarked media in the style of an editorial or objective journalistic article. To entice prospective buyers into purchasing a product, direct marketers present offers they bill as "free trials". In order for a prospective buyer to receive a "free trial" they are required to submit their personal information and as well as credit card to handle "shipping and handling" of the free product they are expecting to receive.

DATA COLLECTION AND ORDER PROCESSING

Once the consumer enters their personal and credit card information, the order is processed and sent to a fulfillment center for shipping. In addition to the standard $4.95 shipping rate consumers believe they are paying for, they are typically auto-enrolled in a product subscription program wherein their credit card is billed monthly or until they contact the seller to cancel. Another malicious tactic used by sellers charges the consumers credit card for a 3-month supply of a product when the free-trial transaction is processed. The 3-month supply often exceeds $150 in cost, which goes directly to the buyer's credit card. In order to cancel the order, the consumer must contact the seller to dispute the charge. Some high volume sellers employ call centers whose sole responsibility is credit card disputes and mitigation. This is to ensure that their phone lines are not clogged when new customers phone in to process new product orders.

WHITE LABEL PRODUCTS AND FULFILLMENT

It is easy to create and distribute a unique brand of health supplements, as the industry is largely unregulated. There are a number of companies that manufacture health supplements to seller specification. The bottles can be prepared without labels and in any bottle the seller specifies. This means that sellers have tremendous flexibility with the offers they present. If one brand of product isn't moving, they can simply change the name of the product and reprint new labels. The fulfillment companies that process the orders and ship the orders often ship from off-site UPS shipping centers. This is often the return address listed on the mailing labels used in place of any authentically registered business address.

TRUSTED PARTNERS AND AFFILIATED COMPANIES

This vicious and deceptive consumer cycle is perpetuated by people and companies that with innate knowledge of ongoing regulation efforts and a firm understanding of where the gaps in online governance and compliance are. Techniques and business models that prove lucrative quickly become industry standard. Competitors in the direct marketing space will blatantly steal the media and design elements that are successfully deceiving consumers and converting new buyers on competitive sites for use on their own landing pages and offers. Expert direct marketers easily identify which players and resources are essential to a product offer that is successful and lucrative.

When someone proves proficient or technically skilled in one element of the operation, they are revered and sought after. Their ideas become new standards for online direct marketers.

EVADING ENFORCEMENT

Marketers can register a fly-by-night LLC in Delaware, establish a drop shipment address at a UPS shipping center, update digital marketing materials, print new product labels and invest considerable financial resources into marketing a new product offer in a matter of days. The illegal aspect of their operation that first got our attention is unwarranted use of our trademark in their marketing materials, but we are most concerned with the consumer being misled. Most direct marketers will only leverage our trademark in the advertorial page that appears before a consumer submits their personal and credit card information. The advertorial pages are often hosted on "bulletproof" servers with private domain registration in place. Because marketers are able to evade enforcement by concealing their identity when a domain host sends a trademark claim to their attention, they simply repeat the process.

In summary, a direct marketer establishes a connection with a potential buyer via traditional advertising or direct marketing. When the potential buyer clicks a link, they are funneled into a conversion cycle that is laden with unauthorized trademarked material on advertorial pages designed to elicit an immediate action from the buyer. All links on the advertorial page link directly to a product landing page and data capture form.

Proposed Solutions and Suggestions

The uncontrolled proliferation of illicit advertising of weight-loss scams on the Internet is a large scale orchestrated criminal fraud that amounts to hundreds of million of dollars in illegal profits and a grave threat to the health of any person buying and ingesting products from a dishonest seller. There has been a paucity of enforcement of existing laws on the quality and safety of the products, the method of billing which results in fraud or theft by deception, and the rampant and constant trademark infringement. If ever there were an opportunity and an urgency to protect the consumer, this is it.

I believe that we have existing laws that allow for the enforcement of these scams. I believe the power of this committee is critical in shedding light on the situation and raising its level of priority with the appropriate enforcement agencies. I do not think additional regulation or oversight is necessary.

Here are my suggestions as a starting point to deal with this problem:

- Initiate greater intra-agency cooperation between the FTC, FDA, FBI, Congress and State Attorney General offices and the private sector companies (via trade organizations) to identify offenders and shut them down.
- Development of a "master list" of celebrity endorsements retained by the FTC for quick identification of violators. This would be of great assistance to the celebrities who have no practical recourse for trademark infringement and enable the FTC and law enforcement to look in the obvious places in an effort to protect the consumer.
- Web hosting and Internet advertising platforms must bear some responsibility for hosting egregious and obvious false ads or criminal content. A master list would be a useful tool and if developed, ad hosting services could be expected to cross reference celebrity content and expected to refuse purchases for violators as well as report the purchaser.

It's my hope that we leave today with a commitment to cooperate in protecting the consumer. You have my absolute commitment to provide whatever I can that will be of assistance in any of your efforts or with any of the agencies you deem appropriate. I also will continue my earnest efforts to be a public advocate on this issue and use the power of my show and various media platforms to keep it in the public eye.

Thank you for the opportunity to testify.

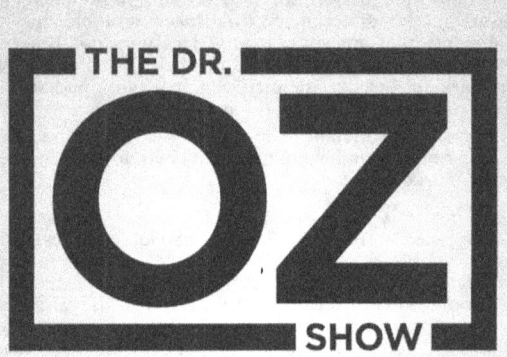

Protecting the Consumer

2012-2014

Prepared By: Oz Digital
Last Updated: June 2014

What People Are Selling

- Green Coffee Bean Extract
- Phytocermides
- Garcina Cambogia
- African Mango Extract
- Garcina Cambogia
- Saffron Extract
- Chitosan
- Forskolin
- Turmeric - Curcumin
- Yacon Syrup
- Red Palm
- Raspberry Ketones

How They're Selling It...

- **Online Banner Ads:** Ad Networks (SiteScout, AdSense), etc.
- **Ad Word Buys:** Google, Facebook, etc.
- **Direct Marketing:** Email, Text, Phone, SMS
- **E-commerce:** Amazon, EBay, various nutrition storefronts, etc.
- **Social Media:** YouTube, Facebook, Twitter, Pinterest
- **Broadcast/Traditional Media:** Television, Radio, Magazines

---

"Making Millions Through Nutrition"

Video Credit: Pace Lattin: http://www.youtube.com/watch?v=9zMlOrRkpAM

More Ads Featuring Dr. Oz or TDOS

Dr Oz: "Mom's $4 Wrinkle Tip"

Kill a bit of your wrinkles everyday by following this 1 old weird tip ▶

" Last Night Dr Oz Spoke About Green Coffee Beans & How They Can Help You Lose Weight "

Order Now

Dr OZ: "Better than a facelift"

Could this be the end of Botox? Hailed as "the secret to cheat your age." Reduce your wrinkles today. Read More

Oprah Looks 29

Lose 21 lbs in 1 Week?

"Miracle Pill Burns Fat FAST!" ▶

Demi Moore Looks 29

Dr OZ:"Better than a facelift" ▶

Dr OZ:"Better than a facelift" ▶

More Ads Featuring Dr. Oz or TDOS

Doctors Banned this Video ▶

55 Year Old Ellen Looks 25

Dr OZ:"Better than a facelift" ▶

Featured on the Dr. OZ Show!

Can You Cure HEART DISEASE?

Shocking video reveals why America's top doctors claim this weird ingredient may stop Heart Disease dead in it's tracks [video]

" Raspberry Ketone Max For Fast & Effective Weight Loss "

Order Now

Eat THIS, Never Diet Again

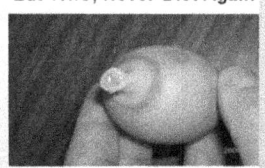

Dr OZ:"The Holy Grail of weight loss" ▶

Use Case 1: Standard Banner Advertisement

User Action: Click advertisement featuring Dr. Oz, land on "advertorial", click through to "Buy Now" landing page

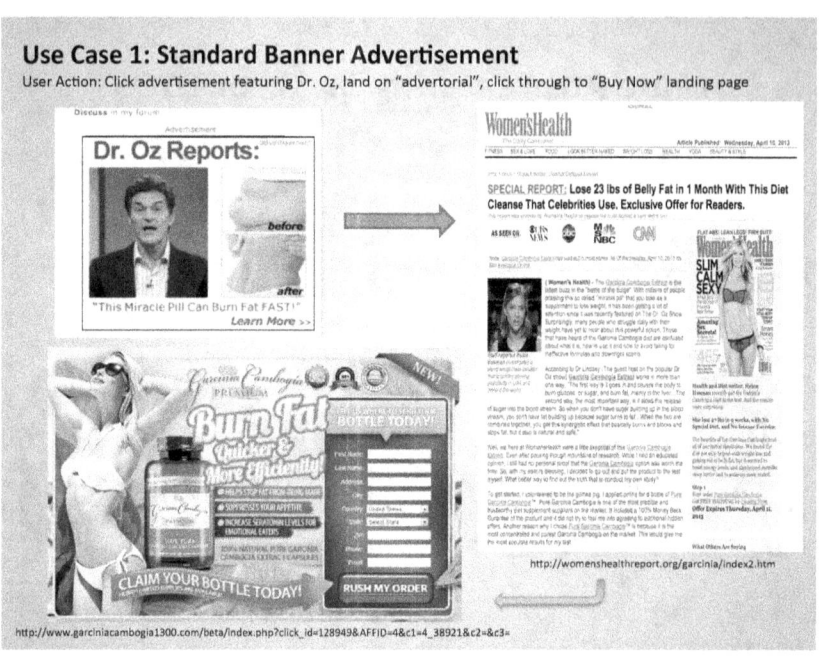

What is an Advertorial?

A newspaper or magazine advertisement giving information about a product in the style of an editorial or objective journalistic article.

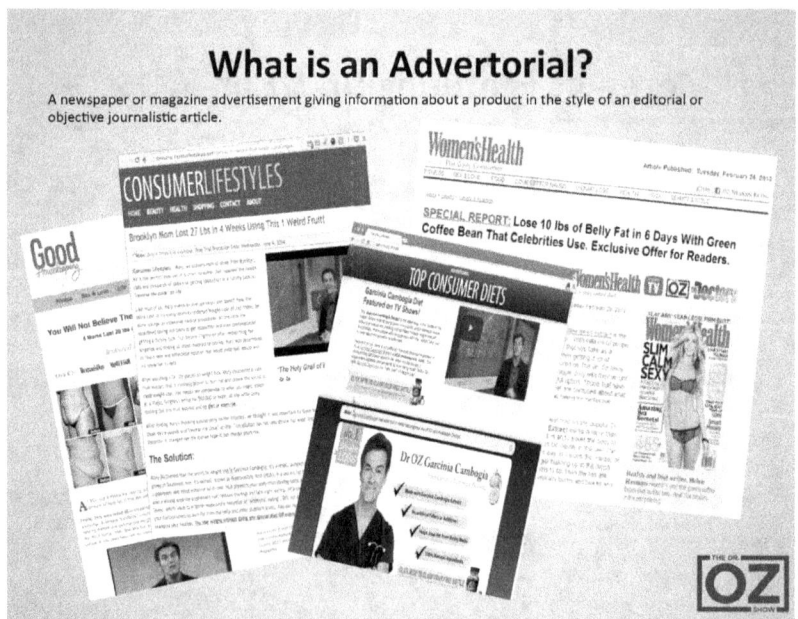

Use Case 2: Paid Ad Words (Google, Yahoo, Bing, etc.)
User Action: Conduct general search, click ad, land on "advertorial", click through to "free trial" landing page

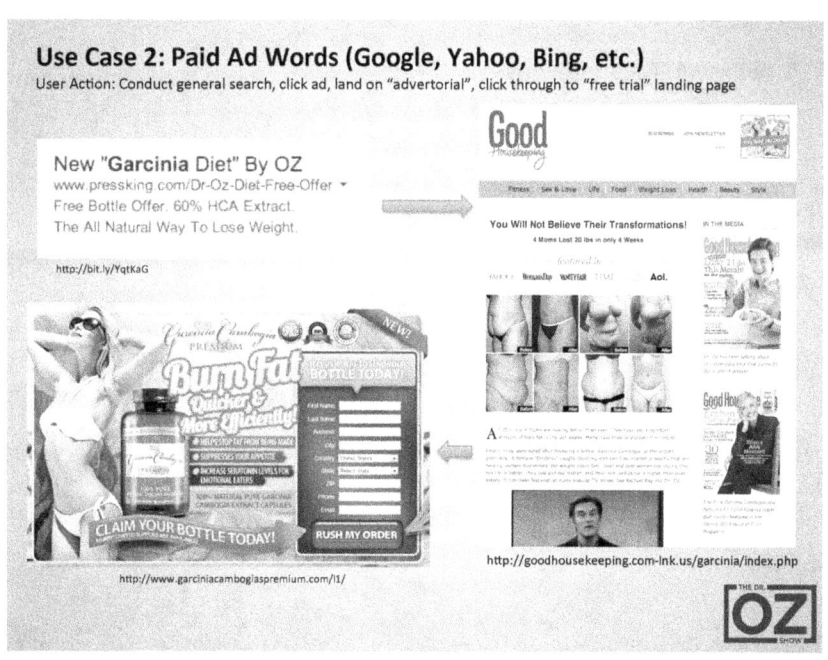

Use Case 3: Email (Direct Marketing)
User Action: Click email link; land on "advertorial", click through to "free trial" landing page

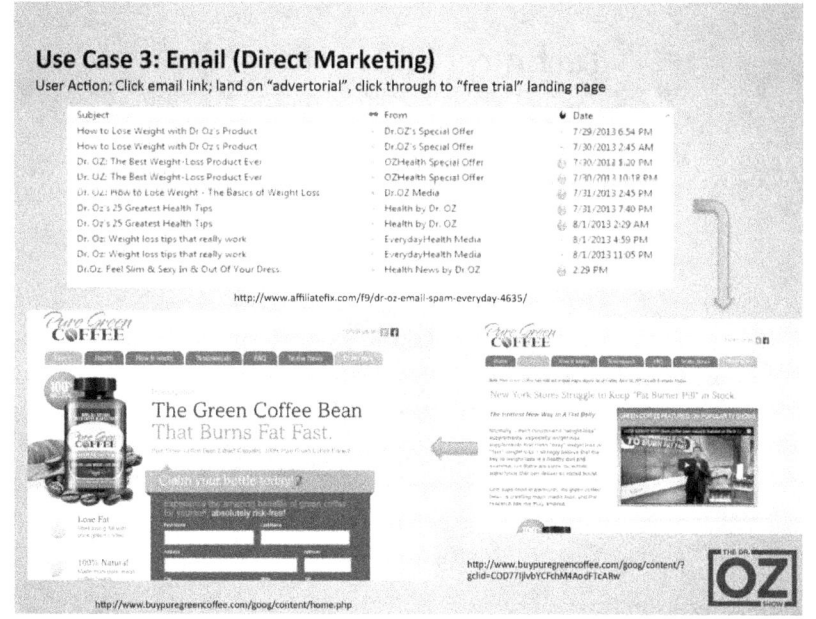

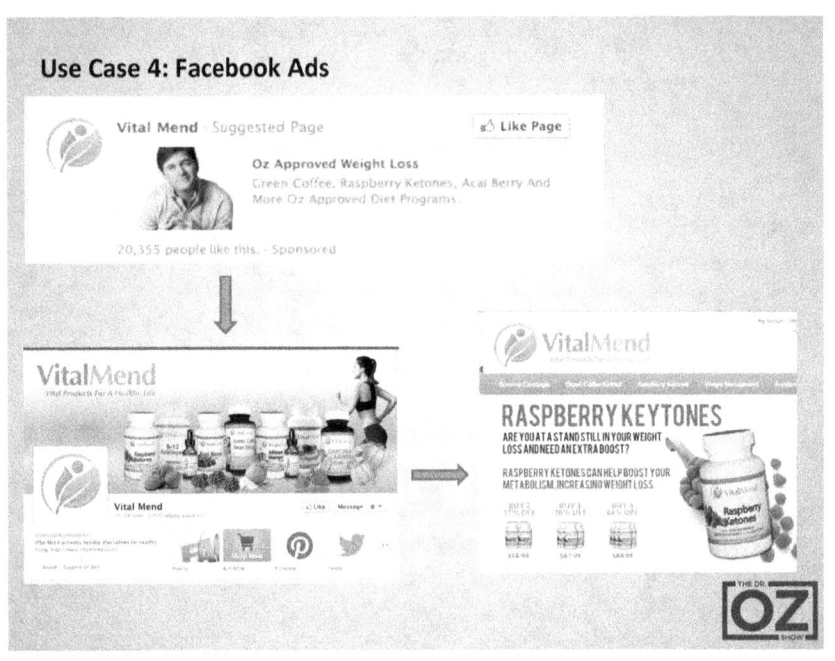

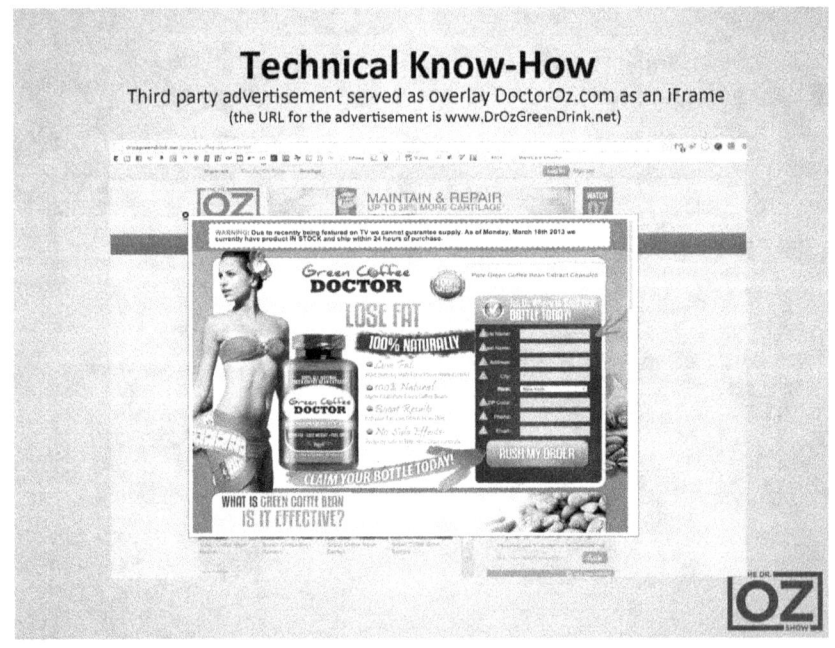

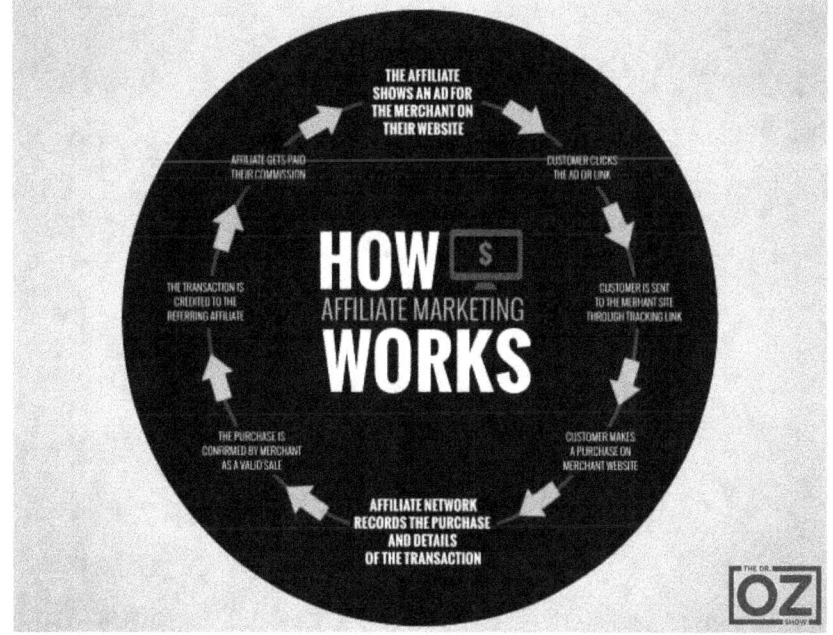

Cornerstones of Successful Affiliate Marketing

- **Expert Direct Marketers:**
  - *"Designed to elicit an immediate response from consumers"*
  - Leverage user-driven ad words and direct telecommunications
  - Possess sizable advertising budget (ad words aren't cheap)
- **Web Development and Strategy:**
  - Domain registration, creative elements/messaging/graphics, site development, data capture system, Search Engine Optimization/Specialists
  - Affiliate Offer, Advertorial landing page (featuring celebrities, mainstream media brands)
- **CRM Solution:**
  - The backend; where the data is stored, how the transactions are processed, where the orders are sent, who gets paid, etc. (LimeLight CRM seems to be best in class)
- **White Label Manufacturer:**
  - Create your own brand; specify product formula, order product, print your own labels
- **Product Fulfillment Center:**
  - International drop shipment, call centers
- **Content Creators:** SEO specialists (page spinners), social media managers, writers, publicists
- **Call Center:** a toll-free call center to process orders; they often can't reference the site their product is sold on or the brand you are attempting to order.
- **Credit Card Mitigation Center:** a team dedicated to credit card claim disputes

How We Responded

Oz Watch: Timeline + Key Metrics

9/12/2009: Dr. Oz and Oprah Winfrey file civil suit against merchants using their likeness to sell and promote acai berry
9/03/2012: Dr. Oz Announces *Oz Watch* "If you see something, send something"
9/12/2012: "Dr. Oz Fights to Reclaim His Name" Show
5/06/2013: Dr. Oz Announces the "It's Not Me" Campaign
4/29/2014: "Dr. Oz Takes Down the Scammers" Show

Total Cases Reported to Oz Watch through 5/31/2014: 35,000+
- "High Value" Targets (image/logo/video infringements) identified: 9,000+
  - Many reported offenses (thousands) are duplicates. This number excludes social media
- **C&Ds sent to date: 600** (not including YouTube and Facebook takedowns) to 450+ sites
  - Sites taken down + Infringements removed in response to C&D: 300+
  - C&Ds sent that produced no result: 78
  - Average Claims Submitted to Oz Watch Per Day: 50
  - Total YouTube Takedowns to Date: 4,700+ videos
  - Total SPAM Messages Reported: 28,000+

General breakdown by claim type (not exact):
- Online: Website, Facebook, Amazon: 62%
- Email/Text: 28%
- Other (Television/Radio/Print): 9%
- In-store: 1 %

May 2013: Public Awareness Effort - "It's Not Me"

Dr. Oz's *"It's Not Me"* Message

Since May 6, 2013, Dr. Oz has ended each show with the following disclaimer

*"If you receive an e-mail or any kind of direct marketing claiming to be from me selling a product with my name, my image or the show's name, you need to know **IT'S NOT ME!** I consider anyone that uses my name or my picture to try to sell you a product or supplement reckless and dangerous. They are undermining my credibility with you and the trust you place in me. More importantly, it could be dangerous to your health.*

Please go to www.DoctorOz.com/oz-watch to report if you receive any messages that use me to sell you anything.

To see a list of our trusted partners, please go to www.DoctorOz.com."

Brand Protection: Mark Monitor

Hired MarkMonitor: October 2013
 — MarkMonitor tracks online use of our brand and sends legal enforcements.

Websites and Paid Search:
- Website Domain Detections: 2,055 results
- Website Content Detections: 4,521 results
- **Enforcements Sent:** 493 to 341 sites (77% compliant rate)
  - 33% of the enforcements were in response to *OzWatch* submissions.

Online Marketplaces: (Amazon, eBay, Craigslist, etc.)
- Marketplace Detections: 2,306 detections
- Enforcements Sent: 2,145

Dr. Oz's Call to Action

- Initiate greater intra-agency cooperation between the FTC, FDA, FBI, Congress and State Attorney General offices and the private sector companies (via trade organizations) to identify offenders and shut them down.

- Development of a private sector voluntary "master registry" of celebrity endorsements retained by the advertising platforms (online and traditional) for quick identification of violators. This would be of great assistance to the celebrities who have no practical recourse for trademark infringement and enable the FTC and law enforcement to look in the obvious places.

- A master registry would be a useful tool and if developed, ad hosting services could be expected to cross reference celebrity content and expected to refuse purchases for violators as well as report the purchaser. This would streamline the process and provide a level of accountability for platforms who are making money selling space to scammers.

Senator MCCASKILL. Thank you, Dr. Oz.
Mr. Peeler

STATEMENT OF C. LEE PEELER, PRESIDENT AND CHIEF EXECUTIVE OFFICER, ADVERTISING SELF-REGULATORY COUNCIL; EXECUTIVE VICE PRESIDENT, ADVERTISING SELF-REGULATION, COUNCIL OF BETTER BUSINESS BUREAUS

Mr. PEELER. Thank you, and good morning. I appreciate the opportunity to testify on the ongoing work of the advertising industry's self-regulatory system, particularly as it applies to weight-loss advertising.

This system was created in 1971 by the Nation's leading advertising trade associations, in cooperation with the Council of Better Business Bureaus. Since that time, we have pioneered a rigorous form of self-regulation that is impartial—it is administered by the Council of Better Business Bureaus. It is comprehensive—it applies to all national advertisers in all media. It's transparent—all of our decisions are publicly reported. And it's effective—companies that do not participate in the process, or don't follow our recommendations, are publicly referred to the appropriate government agency, usually the Federal Trade Commission.

We work on a case-by-case basis, actively monitoring national advertising for questionable claims and practices, and we apply FTC-type standards to those claims. Each year, we issue almost 200 decisions on a wide variety of advertising issues, including about a dozen last year that addressed advertising of weight-loss claims and required the company to stop or modify the ads in question.

Self-regulatory claims for weight-loss products include issues ranging from technical, easy-to-remedy disclosure questions to questions about the validity of complex underlying studies that support the advertiser's claim. For example, one recent NAD decision addressed advertisements for a product called ''Garcinia Cambogia,'' including claims it had been clinically proven to promote four times more weight loss than diet and exercise. Some of the claims were contained in a special report on how to lose 28 pounds in 1 month with two healing cleanses recommended by Dr. Oz. Other claims cited results of specific studies as support for the weight-loss claims. In this case, the advertiser told us that that special report that I referred to earlier was posted by an unauthorized third party, and the advertiser immediately took steps to take the report off the Internet. The NAD determined that the remaining specific product performance claims and ingredients claims should be discontinued in their current form. The advertiser fully cooperated with the review and agreed to discontinue the claims, as do about 90 percent of the companies that participate in the process. We had a very similar case with one of the other ingredients that's popular in this area, Raspberry Ketone.

Our casework complements that of the Better Business Bureau system in protecting consumers. BBBs handle hundreds of advertising review cases locally, including claims associated with weight-loss products and services. BBBs also work to resolve complaints about business practices, and are uniquely positioned to identify local and national scams as they emerge, and warn consumers about them. We are a major outlet for the educational material that the FTC witness described earlier, because we have over 100 Better Business Bureaus located around the country.

Last year, Better Business Bureaus handled thousands of complaints about weight-loss products and services, including a growing number of complaints about weight-loss clinics. BBBs often find that unsubstantiated weight-loss claims are also associated with problematic billing practices and ''autoship'' programs, underscoring the adage that misleading weight-loss claims frequently lighten only the consumer's wallet.

These overall results are consistent with those observed by our St. Louis BBB that serves eastern Missouri and southern Illinois, except that the St. Louis BBB has not seen the rise in the number of weight-loss clinic ads in that particular jurisdiction.

Self-regulation works only if it has the support of the industry and the government. In the area of weight loss, two associations in particular, the Electronic Retailing Association and the Council for Responsible Nutrition, have stepped forward to provide the types of no-strings-attached funding that allows us to do our impartial monitoring and decisionmaking work. Similarly, although there is no formal relationship between the advertising self-regulation process and the government, decades of support by the Federal Trade Commission have been absolutely critical in the success of the process.

Although there have been significant efforts by the Federal and State government to control unsubstantiated and exaggerated claims, more can be done. One of the things that I think everybody agrees on is, the type of State and Federal enforcement actions that the FTC has been bringing. Those are critical to controlling this type of advertising.

In addition, trade associations whose members include representatives of weight-loss industries need to follow the example set by the Electronic Retailing Association and the Council for Responsible Nutrition, and step up and support increased self-regulatory monitoring of the marketplace. It's good for businesses. It's good for consumers.

Finally, the FTC's renewed effort to enlist consistent support of the media in guarding against the most egregious types of weight-loss claims is a key step. Network broadcasters, for example, have fairly sophisticated processes for network ads. And similarly, in the new media, Google has recently introduced a new approach to ad screening that's tailored to that specific new media. But, there are lots of other media outlets—independent TV channels, cable television, satellite radio, and radio—that are not doing as much.

And finally, I guess I'd just close with an anecdote. Just this weekend, I got a spam e-mail. It was for a product called ''Forskolin.'' It said if I took the product, I would never have to diet again. And when I went on the Internet and used Google Earth, I found that the return address was for a post office box. So, it was sort of a regulatory trifecta. It was a spam e-mail, for a ''red flag'' claim that no one can substantiate, with a seller that nobody could find.

Thank you.

[The prepared statement of Mr. Peeler follows:]

PREPARED STATEMENT OF C. LEE PEELER, PRESIDENT AND CEO, ADVERTISING SELF-REGULATORY COUNCIL EXECUTIVE VICE PRESIDENT, ADVERTISING SELF-REGULATION COUNCIL OF BETTER BUSINESS BUREAUS (ASRC)

I appreciate the opportunity to describe for the Subcommittee the ongoing work of the advertising industry's system of self-regulation, particularly as it applies to weight-loss advertising.

According to a recent Gallup poll,[1] 51 percent of American consumers want to lose weight. Weight-loss products come in all sizes and flavors: pills, creams, patches, diets and devices—to name a few. Weight-loss products and fads have long been ubiquitous and popular with consumers. They are, therefore, a primary subject of advertising self-regulatory review proceedings. Current concerns about the Nation's spiraling obesity rates can make unsubstantiated or exaggerated claims of effortless weight loss even more appealing to consumers than in the past. And that means it is even more important to have a process for separating truthful claims about effective products from exaggerated, unsupported or outright false claims about products that don't work.

Advertising Self-Regulatory Council (ASRC)

The advertising industry's self-regulatory system was created in 1971 when three leading advertising trade organizations—the 4A's, American Advertising Federation (AAF) and Association of National Advertisers (ANA)—together with the Council of Better Business Bureaus (CBBB), announced a new alliance to promote truthful and accurate advertising. That alliance, now called the Advertising Self-Regulatory Council or ASRC, sets policies and procedures for advertising industry self-regulation. In addition to the founding partners, the ASRC Board now includes the chief executives of the Electronic Retailing Association (ERA) and Interactive Advertising Bureau (IAB), giving ASRC significant reach throughout the advertising and marketing community.

[1] *Americans' Desire to Shed Pounds Outweighs Effort*
http://www.gallup.com/poll/166082/americans-desire-shed-pounds-outweighs-effort.aspx

Advertising Self-Regulation

ASRC has pioneered a unique form of self-regulation. Our programs, described in Appendix A, are:

- Impartial and administered by a third party—the Council of Better Business Bureaus.
- Comprehensive—they apply to all national advertisers in all media
- Transparent—all decisions are public both for guidance to the industry and to ensure public accountability.
- Effective—although the self-regulatory system is voluntary, there are consequences for non-participation or non-compliance, including public referral to the appropriate government agency, usually the Federal Trade Commission (FTC).

Administration by the Council of Better Business Bureaus (CBBB)

To ensure the impartiality and independence of the self-regulatory process, the system is administered by the CBBB. The CBBB is the network hub for the Better Business Bureau system in the United States and Canada, which works to promote trust in the marketplace.

Operation of the Self-Regulatory System

All ASRC programs operate on a standard model. While the programs accept challenges and resolve disputes between competing advertisers, they also actively monitor national advertising for questionable claims or practices that may violate industry guidelines [2] or principles.[3]

Active monitoring is particularly important in the weight-loss area where consumers are often reluctant to complain and may attribute poor results from the products to themselves, rather than to the product.

Staff monitoring is supplemented by a robust competitor challenge process. As the United States Supreme Court observed last week: ''Competitors who manufacture or distribute products have detailed knowledge regarding how consumers rely on certain sales and marketing strategies. Their awareness of unfair competition practices may be far more immediate and accurate than that of agency rulemakers and regulators.'' [4]

By providing a fast, expert forum to resolve these complaints and a transparent public record of the resolution, ASRC programs harness this expertise to serve the interests of the public.

Self-regulatory cases for weight-loss products may involve a range of issues from technical and easy-to-remedy disclosure questions, to questions about the validity of complex underlying studies. In some cases, we recommend that the advertiser make certain modifications to the advertising. In others, we may recommend discontinuance of the entire ad. If an advertisement is the subject of an FTC order, court order or ongoing litigation we will advise the parties that the complaint is not, or is no longer, appropriate for investigation in this forum.

When a self-regulatory inquiry is opened, the advertiser is asked to provide its support for a questioned claim. The advertiser's support for the claim is reviewed by skilled attorney staff, who then issue a decision that analyzes the claims made in the ad, the advertiser's support (substantiation) for the claims and the fit between the two.

The advertising self-regulatory process is both similar to and different from government enforcement. It applies the same standards for claim substantiation as the FTC, but it does not have subpoena power to compel the production of documents and relies on evidence voluntarily produced by the parties. The self-regulatory process is comparatively short. Both the National Advertising Division (NAD) and Electronic Retailing Self-Regulation Program (ERSP) strive to resolve cases in 60 to 90 days.

Overall, the self-regulatory system issues roughly 200 decisions each year. While there are no sanctions (penalties, redress, etc.) beyond requiring discontinuance or modification of advertising, the relative time-to-decision makes self-regulation a very valuable addition to the existing government regulatory framework for adver-

---

[2] *Self-Regulatory Program for Children's Advertising*
http://www.asrcreviews.org/wp-content/uploads/2012/04/Guidelines-FINAL-FINAL-RE-VISED-20142.pdf
[3] *The DAA Self-Regulatory Principles*
http://www.aboutads.info/principles
[4] *Pom Wonderful LLC* v. *Coca-Cola Co.*
Supreme Court of the United States, Slip Opinion at page 11–12, June 12, 2014

tising. It helps ensure that industry members comply with strong standards and frees government resources to focus on the most egregious cases. Overall, more than 90 percent of advertisers voluntarily participate in the program and make recommended changes to their advertising.

Funding for Self-Regulation

The advertising-self regulatory system is funded entirely by the advertising industry through the sales of products and services—including dispute resolution services and online access to self-regulatory decisions—national partnerships with the CBBB and direct funding of programs through trade associations.

FTC Support for Self-Regulation

During more than 40 years of practice, the advertising self-regulatory system has received strong support from the FTC.[5]

Although there is no formal relationship between the government and the self-regulatory system, the FTC's ongoing support for self-regulation contributes meaningfully to the success of the process. Referrals to the FTC of advertisers that refused to participate in the self-regulatory process have resulted in FTC lawsuits and significant monetary penalties.[6]

Further, FTC guidance on advertising issues, including the "FTC Guides Concerning the Use of Endorsement and Testimonials in Advertising," "Dietary Supplement Advertising Guidelines" and its recently published "Gut Check: A Reference Guide for Media on Spotting False Weight Loss Claims," provides valuable counsel for advertisers and self-regulatory bodies. The FTC's guidance is further enforced through the decisions of the self-regulatory system, which applies FTC standards to its review of specific ads.

Better Business Bureau Advertising Reviews

The work of the national advertising self-regulatory programs complements the role of the Better Business Bureau (BBB) system in protecting consumers. BBBs maintain active advertising monitoring programs in their communities under the BBB Code of Advertising. BBBs handle hundreds of advertising review cases, including pricing claims, inadequate disclosures and qualifications, superiority claims, rebates and warranty and guarantee claims.

BBBs also work to resolve complaints about business practices and are in a unique position to identify potential scams—both locally and nationally—and warn consumers about fraud. BBBs also have excellent access to the media outlets in their communities.

The BBB notes that more than 4,300 complaints about weight-loss supplements were filed nationwide in 2013, including complaints about paying for but not receiving merchandise, refund and exchange issues and potentially misleading claims.

The BBB system, which makes its ratings and business reviews available to all consumers, can provide consumers a resource by allowing them to check a company's complaint history before making a purchase.

Complaint data from the BBB system is shared with both Federal and state law enforcement agencies. In fact, complaints from the BBB system makes up more than

[5] *"Truth or Consequences: The FTC Approach to Advertising"*
Remarks of Commissioner Jon Leibowitz at The National Advertising Division Annual Conference—September 24, 2007

"All of us at the FTC appreciate the NAD's advertising review work. It is more important today than it has ever been.. . .It really helps to have an alternative procedure that is quick, fair, and well-respected." http://www.ftc.gov/speeches/leibowitz/070924bbbremarks.pdf

The Federal Trade Commission at 100: Into Our Second Century
The Continuing Pursuit of Better Practices: A Report by Federal Trade Commission Chairman William E. Kovacic—January 2009.

"Meaningful self-regulation is an important complement to the Commission's law enforcement efforts—particularly in the area of deceptive marketing practices. For example, the program administered by the National Advertising Division/National Advertising Review Council ("ASRC") arm of the Council of Better Business Bureaus ("CBBB") has worked well to obviate the need for Commission action in some instances." http://www.ftc.gov/ftc/workshops/ftc100/docs/ftc100rpt.pdf.

Self-Regulation in the Infomercial Industry:
Deborah Platt Majoras, Chairman, Federal Trade Commission
Before the Electronic Retailing Self-Regulation Program—April 2006
(Footnote No. 3, listing FTC statements in support of self-regulation since 1978.)
http://www.ftc.gov/speeches/majoras/060503eraspeech.pdf.
[6] *Court Orders Spammers to Give Up $3.7 Million*
http://www.ftc.gov/opa/2009/07/spear.shtm   ;

20 percent of the data in the FTC Consumer Sentinel fraud detection database and information from complaints filed with BBBs is often used by Federal and state law enforcement agencies to build cases, including cases against companies that sell bogus weight-loss products.

Advertising Self-Regulation and Weight-loss Claims

Truthful and substantiated advertising for weight-loss products, diets and exercise devices that work can be of substantial assistance to consumers seeking to achieve and maintain a healthy weight.

Misleading, unsubstantiated or exaggerated advertising claims—often for products promising quick, effortless weight loss—have the opposite effect, causing both health and economic injury to consumers.

In addition to harm done to consumers, these types of claims also injure honest competitors who promote effective products and whose ads acknowledge the difficulty consumers may face in losing weight and sustaining weight loss.

Misleading advertising both misappropriates sales that would otherwise go to legitimate products and services and undermines the credibility of advertising generally, making it more expensive for honest advertisers to reach their audiences. Recognizing these twin harms, two industry trade associations—The Electronic Retailing Association (ERA) and the Council for Responsible Nutrition (CRN)—have stepped forward to fund impartial monitoring and oversight of advertising claims, including a substantial number of weight-loss claims.

In 2004, the ERA funded the development of the ERSP program, which provides independent monitoring of all direct-response advertising for a wide range of products, including weight-loss products.

Since its founding, the ERSP program has issued more than 350 decisions, often requiring modification or discontinuance of the challenged advertising. Almost one-third of all ERSP cases have involved weight-loss claims.

In 2006, CRN provided the National Advertising Division with funding for an attorney who would concentrate on monitoring advertising claims for dietary supplements. Since 2006, NAD, through this initiative, has examined advertising claims made for 164 separate supplements, including 30 weight-loss products.

Although the majority of advertisers comply with the recommendations of the self-regulatory system, those who decline to participate in an ERSP or NAD review or refuse to implement recommended changes are referred to the most appropriate Federal regulatory agency, most often the FTC.

Current Issues in Weight-Loss Advertising

While diet fads come and go, certain troublesome claims regularly appear, including claims that a supplement is ''clinically proven'' to work or is ''doctor recommended.'' Claims that state or imply that products will provide fast, effortless weight loss without any changes to diet or exercise are published over and over again. (Appendix B: Weight-Loss Claims Digest)

It is not uncommon to find that a product has not been tested or that the results of testing on a product's ingredients do not support the advertiser's claims. Although the FTC's 2009 revisions to the ''Endorsements and Testimonial Guides'' have improved compliance, unsupported testimonials from ''real users'' and misleading ''before'' and ''after'' pictures remain a significant concern.

Some media, like the major national broadcast television networks, and some new media like Google, have relatively sophisticated advertising clearance and screening processes. Others do not, and should be called upon to implement effective screening protocols, particularly for weight-loss products. Such screening is good for consumers, for honest advertisers and for the media in general.

Meanwhile, the volume of media channels available to promote products has exploded, along with the use of ''affiliate marketing'' in which multiple sellers make—and often elaborate on—claims made for weight-loss products like acai berry and green coffee products. Products promoted by unsubstantiated or exaggerated claims are often marketed through spam e-mails and all marketers are increasingly using social media –Pinterest, for example—to promote their products.

For example, a recent NAD decision addressed claims made for a product called Garcinia Cambogia Formula, including claims that the product had been clinically proven to promote four times more weight loss than diet and exercise.

Some of the claims were contained in a ''Special Report'' on how to lose 28 lbs. in one month with products recommended by Dr. Oz.

Other claims included:

- ''It's scientifically proven to tear away fat from your body. In studies taken out by renowned health research institution Queens University in Canada, Garcinia

Cambogia was proven to ignite your metabolism and therefore fat burning capabilities by around 300 percent when taken regularly.''

The advertiser asserted that the ''Special Report'' and claims made in that report were posted by an unauthorized third party and immediately took steps to have the report taken off the Internet.

This now deleted ''Special Report'' appeared to be a ''fake'' news report similar to advertisements by acai berry supplement manufacturers promising rapid and dramatic weight loss that were the subject of FTC enforcement actions in recent years.

NAD determined that the remaining product performance and ingredient claims promising weight and fat loss should be discontinued based on the lack of reliable scientific evidence demonstrating that the product, or its ingredients, elicit the claimed benefits. The advertiser fully cooperated in the review and agreed to discontinue the claims reviewed by NAD.

Additionally, we have seen—and taken action against—the use of seemingly independent diet product review sites that are in fact controlled by marketers. (For example, one marketer operated a diet-review site that stated: ''there are now literally thousands of weight-loss products and diet programs available to choose from . . . Our goal is to give you a quick snapshot of what options are available to you.'')

Finally, BBB advertising review programs from around the country indicate consumer complaints and ad review issues focusing on weight-loss clinics.

The BBB notes that weight-loss products and programs (like weight-loss clinics) marketed with exaggerated or unsubstantiated claims are often also associated with problematic billing practices, poorly or entirely undisclosed negative option ''auto ship'' plans and a failure to make refunds for returned products.

While BBB notes that overall complaints about negative-option shipping issues are decreasing and are not limited only to weight-loss supplements, complaints regarding the practice remain significant.

Recommendations

Although there have been significant efforts by federal, state and self-regulatory organizations to control unsubstantiated, exaggerated and misleading claims in the weight-loss marketplace, more can done.

State and Federal enforcement actions are critically important and support the self-regulatory system by underscoring for companies working in the weight-loss marketplace the seriousness of these claims.

Trade associations whose members include representatives of weight-loss industries should follow the example set by ERA and CRN and step up to support self-regulation of the marketplace. Experience shows self-regulation can be an effective tool in producing prompt, voluntary compliance by many advertisers. That is good for honest competitors in the weight-loss industry and it is good for consumers.

The FTC's renewed effort to enlist the consistent support of the media in guarding against the most egregious weight-loss claims is key, as well. Guidance from both the FTC and the self-regulatory system is public and available for review.

Small- and medium-sized media outlets may not be able to conduct the detailed review of weight-loss advertising claims that NAD and ERSP apply, but they can 5 and should check the advertisements they accept for publication against the very straightforward screening criteria suggested by the FTC, review the ads against self-regulatory decisions already published by the ASRC and check the advertiser's complaint history with the BBB.

These steps aren't foolproof, but collectively they help bleed false and misleading claims from the weight-loss marketplace, level the playing field for honest advertisers and help bolster consumer confidence in advertising.

38

APPENDIX A: ADVERTISING INDUSTRY SELF-REGULATION IN BRIEF

Advertising Industry Self-Regulation

Advertising Industry Self-Regulation has pioneered the use of independent, transparent oversight to assure compliance with industry standards. More than 90 percent of advertisers who participate in the advertising industry's system of self-regulation voluntarily comply with its decisions. Failure to participate or to comply with decisions results in public referral to the appropriate government agency.

The Advertising Self-Regulatory Council is the governing body for advertising self-regulation. ASRC's 11-member Board of Directors is comprised of the top leadership of the 4A's, American Advertising Federation (AAF), Association of National Advertisers (ANA), Council of Better Business Bureaus (CBBB), Electronic Retailing Association (ERA) and Interactive Advertising Bureau (IAB).

The Self-Regulatory Programs:

- NAD—The National Advertising Division (NAD) monitors national advertising in all media, enforcing high standards of truth and accuracy. NAD examines advertising claims made for goods and services as diverse and critical as telecommunications, infant nutrition, over-the-counter medications and dietary supplements and ''green'' products. NAD accepts complaints from consumers, competing advertisers and local Better Business Bureaus. NAD's decisions represent the single largest body of advertising decisions in the U.S.

   In addition to its own monitoring, NAD provides a fast, expert forum for the resolution of competitors' disputes. NAD handles about 150 cases each year and publicly reports its formal decisions.

- NAD/CRN—Created in cooperation with the Council for Responsible Nutrition, the NAD/CRN program has expanded NAD's review of advertising for dietary supplements, a nearly $35 billion industry.

- Accountability Program—Developed in cooperation with the Digital Advertising Alliance (DAA), the Online Interest-Based Advertising Accountability Program is charged with ensuring industry compliance with the Self-Regulatory Principles for Online Behavioral Advertising (Principles). The Principles require third parties to provide consumers with an easy-to-use mechanism that allows the consumer to exercise choice regarding the collection and use of data from their device for online behavioral advertising (OBA) purposes. The Accountability Program announced its first formal decisions in November 2011.

- CARU—Recognizing the special vulnerability of young children, the Children's Advertising Review Unit (CARU) holds advertisers to a high standard of truth and appropriateness when they direct advertising to young children. Among other things, CARU's guidelines provide that advertisers can not state or imply that their products will make children more popular with their peers, advertise vitamins or other products that carry ''keep out of reach of children'' labels, or advertise products that are unsafe for young children to use. CARU examines advertising in all media, including electronic media, and monitors Websites to assure that they are compliant with CARU's guidelines.

- The Initiative—The Children's Food and Beverage Advertising Initiative (Initiative) is an ASRC-endorsed program, run by the CBBB. The Initiative responds to concerns regarding food advertising to young children. It is comprised of 17 leading food and beverage companies. It promotes the advertising of healthier products in children's media and publishes regular reports on compliance with its principles.

- ERSP—Developed with the Electronic Retailing Association, the Electronic Retailing Self-Regulation Program (ERSP) examines the truth and accuracy of core claims made in electronic direct-response advertising. ERSP monitors the $170 billion direct-response marketplace, providing a strong self-regulatory presence on the frontier of electronic commerce.

- NARB—The National Advertising Review Board is the appellate body of the self-regulatory system. It is made up of industry professionals who hear appeals of decisions by NAD and CARU. NARB panel members are nominated by the ASRC Board of Directors.

ASRC programs are funded through a variety of sources, including through the support of industry associations (ERA, CRN, Digital Advertising Alliance), the direct support of children's advertisers and child-directed media and revenue from the sale of products and services. National Partnerships with the CBBB makes up the remainder.

Self-regulation is good for consumers. The self-regulatory system monitors the marketplace, holds advertisers responsible for their claims and practices and tracks emerging issues and trends.

Self-regulation is good for advertisers. Rigorous review serves to encourage consumer trust; the self-regulatory system offers an expert, cost-efficient, meaningful alternative to litigation and provides a framework for the development of a self-regulatory solution to emerging issues.

To learn more about supporting advertising industry self-regulation, please visit us at: *www.asrcreviews.org.*

APPENDIX B: WEIGHT-LOSS CLAIMS DIGEST

Weight-Loss Claims Digest

The National Advertising Division (NAD) and Electronic Retailing Self-Regulation Program (ERSP) are investigative units of the U.S. advertising industry's system of self-regulation.

NAD seeks to ensure that claims made in national advertising are truthful, accurate and not misleading. NAD requires that objective product performance claims made in advertising be supported by competent and reliable evidence. NAD cases can be initiated through staff monitoring of advertising claims or through "challenges" to advertising claims filed by competitors, consumers, or public-interest groups. NAD also receives a significant number of dietary supplements cases from the Council for Responsible Nutrition (CRN) initiative. CRN, a trade association representing dietary supplement manufacturers, files challenges with NAD to encourage manufacturers to provide substantiation for their advertising claims to ensure that claims are truthful, not misleading and are substantiated with credible scientific evidence.

Since 2006, NAD and the National Advertising Review Board—the appellate arm of the self-regulatory system—have issued more than 30 decisions that specifically addressed claims made for "weight-loss" supplements.

ERSP is responsible for evaluating the truth and accuracy of core claims made in direct response advertising. ERSP inquires about the evidentiary support that a marketer possesses for claims made in direct-response advertising, and determines whether the marketer has provided a reasonable basis for the representations. Advertising comes to the attention of ERSP through its monitoring program, consumers, and challenges from competitors.

While diet fads come and go, certain claims regularly appear in advertising for weight-loss products, including claims that a product is "clinically proven," "doctor recommended," or works without any changes in diet or exercise.

It is not uncommon to find that a product has not been tested or that the results of testing on a product's ingredients do not support the claims made. Unsupported testimonials from "real users" and "before" and "after" pictures remain consistent issues in weight-loss advertising.

Safety Claims

Healthy Life Sciences, LLC
Healthe Trim Weight Loss Dietary Supplements
Case #5641 (10.10.13)

Claim at Issue:

• *Healthe Trim is perfectly safe.*

NAD Findings: The advertiser submitted a 12-week study that demonstrated that, for the duration of the study, the supplement was well-tolerated by the participants. However, the advertiser did not have any long-term studies demonstrating the safety of Healthe Trim after twelve weeks. Further, study participants were required to limit their caffeine consumption to one serving a day or less. NAD recommended that the advertiser modify its safety claim that "Healthe Trim is perfectly safe" to include a reference to the length of time that the safety of Healthe Trim was studied and also that the safety study was conducted on participants who limited their caffeine intake to one serving a day or less. Such disclosures should be prominent and appear in close proximity to the safety claim.

Clinically Proven Claims

Zylotrim, LLC
Zylotrim Weight Loss Supplement
Case #207 (3.4.09)

Claims at Issue:

- *"Clinically proven to more than double the activity of fat burning enzymes"*
- *" "80 percent of each pound that was lost was pure body fat"*
- *"Rated #1 weight loss active ingredient!"*

ERSP Findings: ERSP concluded that the marketer's evidence did not adequately support its claim that Zylotrim is *"clinically proven to more than double the activity of fat burning enzymes"* or that *"80 percent of each pound that was lost was pure body fat"* and recommended that these claims be either modified or discontinued. ERSP also determined that the *"Rated #1 Weight Loss Active Ingredient"* claim is inaccurate and should be either modified or discontinued in the current context in which the claim is presented in the advertising and on the product packaging.

"Before and After" Depictions

Wellnx Life Sciences, Inc.
NV Hollywood Weight-Loss Supplements
Case # 5629 (9.10.13)

The evidence offered in support of advertising claims must mirror the claims in scope and nature.

Claims at issue:

- *Lose weight fast!*
- *Incredible weight-loss power*!
- Claims accompanied by photograph of model Holly Madison, who had lost two jean sizes.

NAD findings: NAD determined that the two clinical trials offered in support of the advertiser's weight-loss claims were methodologically sound in that both of the studies were randomized, double-blind, placebo-controlled studies that utilized the same dosage and form of the two active ingredients found in NV Hollywood. The study participants were obese women.

However, there was no evidence in the record that the model in the advertising—who had not been obese when she began taking NV Hollywood—would achieve the same results in the same time frame. Further, the advertisement did not make reference to the diet and exercise changes that the study participants also underwent to achieve their weight-loss goals. Consequently, NAD recommended that advertiser discontinue its clams that NV Hollywood causes *"fast"* weight loss or has *"incredible weight-loss power."*

Vital Pharmaceutical, Inc.
Meltdown Fat Assault Beverage & Fat Incinerator Capsules
NARB Panel #171 (7.18.11)

"Before" and "after" pictures depicting weight and fat loss are advertising claims that must be supported by competent and reliable evidence demonstrating that they are results a consumer could typically expect to achieve.

Claims at Issue:

- *Product packaging shows (a) "before" and "after" pictures of a woman who lost 21 pounds and reduced her body fat from 23.1 percent to 14.8 percent and (b) "before" and "after" pictures of a man who lost 28 pounds and reduced his body fat from 12.5 percent to 5.27 percent.*

NAD/NARB Findings: The "before" and "after" comparisons reasonably conveyed the message that the depicted weight/fat losses were typical results that consumers could expect to achieve through use of the product.

However, there was nothing in the record to show that the weight/fat losses depicted were what could typically be achieved. Further, there was no evidence to provide a reasonable basis to support a message that use of Meltdown Fat Assault would result in any visible weight or fat loss. NAD/NARB recommended that the advertiser discontinue these "before" and "after" pictures.

Endorsements, Testimonials, Disclosures

Nutrisystem, Inc. (Pinterest)
"Real Consumers. Real Success."
Case # 5479 (6.29.12)

NAD, following its review of "Real Consumers. Real Success."—a Pinterest board maintained by Nutrisystem, Inc.—determined that the weight-loss success stories "pinned" to such boards represent consumer testimonials and require the complete disclosure of material information.

Nutrisystem's "Real Consumers" pinboard featured photos of "real" Nutrisystem customers and highlighted their weight-loss successes. The customer's name, total weight loss and a link to the Nutrisystem website appeared below each photo.

Claims at issue in NAD's review included:

- "Christine B. lost 46lbs on Nutrisystem."
- "Michael H. lost 125 lbs. on Nutrisystem."
- "Lisa M. lost 115 lbs. on Nutrisystem."
- "Christine H. lost 223 lbs. on Nutrisystem."

Upon receipt of NAD's inquiry, the company asserted that necessary disclosures were inadvertently omitted from Pinterest. The advertiser stated that the testimonials at issue had appeared on Pinterest for less than two months, and said the disclosures were added immediately upon receipt of NAD's opening letter. NAD noted its appreciation that Nutrisystem took immediate steps to provide such disclosures.

Liquid HCG Diet, LLC
Liquid HCG Diet
Case #246 (6.16.10)

Claims at Issue:

- *"Lose 30lbs. in a month, it's easy and quick!"*
- *"Burns fat fast"*
- *"Lasting results! Keep it off!"*
- *Becky and husband lost 14lbs in 2 days!"; website claim "Today is my second day on P2 and I lost 5.9lbs. and my husband lost 8lbs.!"*

ERSP Findings: ERSP recommended that the marketer discontinue its weight loss claims in the context in which they are currently communicated and that it modify its use of consumer testimonials in a way that complies with Section 255 of the FTC's revised Guides Concerning the Use of Endorsements and Testimonials in Advertising.

Urban Nutrition, LLC
WeKnowDiets.com (and affiliated websites)
Case #219 (8.11.09)

Claims at Issue:

- *". . . there are now literally thousands of weight loss products and diet programs available to choose from—that can be a little confusing."; "Our goal is to give you a quick snapshot of what options are available to you."*
- *"We have compiled the most comprehensive database of information for people who are looking for a trimmer body and healthier lifestyle."; "We have the largest weight loss database in America."*

ERSP Findings: ERSP determined that the representations made on WeKnowDiets and affiliated websites constituted an advertising message (*i.e.*, a paid commercial message that has the purpose of inducing a sale or other commercial transaction or persuading the audience of the value or usefulness of a company, product or service) and that certain individuals writing favorable product reviews on the website may be considered endorsers. Because Urban Nutrition owned not only the websites at issue, but several products being reviewed on the websites, ERSP concluded that this relationship constituted a *"material connection"* that would not be reasonably expected by the audience and one that would have a significant effect on the weight or credibility given to the endorsement by that audience.

Iovate Health Sciences International
Hydroxycut Nutritional Supplement
Case #70 (1.17.06)

Claims at Issue:

- *"I've reviewed the research. You can lose weight fast, increase energy, and control appetite with Hydroxycut. In my opinion nothing works better or faster."* (Dr. Lydon)
- *"With the science of Hydroxycut, you can lose up to 4.5 times the weight than with diet and exercise alone."*
- *"I lost 29 pounds with Hydroxycut—Hydroxycut can get you in peak shape. With diet and exercise only, you can't really get where you want as quickly. You really need Hydroxycut to speed things up and tighten you up. I quickly lost 29 pounds* [in 8 weeks] *and 5½ inches off my weight using Hydroxycut.*"* (Dr. Marshall)

ERSP Findings: ERSP concluded that Dr. Lydon's claim communicated an unqualified parity claim that was not supported by Iovate. Although Dr. Marshall's testimonial was literally accurate, the fact that two muscle building products supplements were used in addition to Hydroxycut to achieve the results communicated in the advertisement was material information with respect to consumers interpretation of the claims that needed to be more prominently disclosed in the advertising.

Performance Claims

Hollywood Health & Beauty, LTD. Trimbal-EXP200
Case #5112 (4.07.10)

Claims suggesting that you can lose weight without diet and exercise were not supported by reliable scientific evidence.

Claims at Issue:

- *In a few minutes, this amazing capsule expands to become a 100 percent natural gastric balloon.*
- *It attracts, surrounds and absorbs some of the fat, carbohydrates and sugars that you've eaten and they are naturally flushed out without having a chance to be absorbed by your body and converted to excess fat.*
- *"This weight loss plan is 100 percent safe."*
- *The effects were immediate.*
- *I ate everything I liked and as much as I liked.*
- *The first month, I lost exactly 33 pounds without any effort.*
- *The most incredible thing was that my stomach quickly became flat and firm.*
- *I could eat all the foods I like and as much as I wanted.*
- *I lost a total of 48 pounds in 7 weeks.*
- *When you use the Trimball-EXP200 capsule, you are going to eat 2, 3 or even up to 4 times less, as you feel that your stomach is FULL.*
- *You will not experience any feelings of hunger.*
- *You will then automatically lose weight.*
- *These two properties have been confirmed by many clinical studies conducted in the USA by leading dietary researcher, Professor Walsh from the University of Minnesota.*

NAD Findings: The advertiser's supplement contained glucomannan, an ingredient that forms a "bulk" in the stomach by absorbing water and possibly reducing hunger pangs.

The advertiser submitted one small study of 20 obese subjects who took glucomannan fiber and were instructed not to change their eating or exercising habits. Over an 8-week period, the treatment group lost 5.5 pounds.

NAD determined that it was necessary and appropriate for the advertiser to discontinue all of its claims because the study did not support the claims that glucomannan was as effective as gastric bypass surgery, that consumers could eat whatever they liked and still lose weight or that a consumer would typically lose large amounts of weight as claimed.

Further, NAD concluded that this advertising included several claims that have been identified by the FTC "red flags" as bogus weight loss claims, including claims that the product can cause weight loss of more than two pounds a week; works without dieting or exercise; causes substantial weight loss no matter what or how much the consumer eats; blocks the absorption of fat or calories to enable consumers to lose substantial weight; and can safely enable consumers to lose more than three pounds per week for more than four weeks.

Smart for Life Weight Management Centers
Smart for Life Cookies
Case #242 (6.1.10)

Claims at Issue:

- *"Eat Cookies. Lose Weight. It's that simple."*
- *"I lost 105 lbs"* [Lost 105 lbs in 12 months]
- *"I lost 115 lbs in 6 months"* [Lost 115 lbs in 6 months]
- *"Lost 25 lbs in 5 weeks"*

ERSP Findings: ERSP determined that it would not be unreasonable for consumers to take away the message that besides eating the Diet Cookies, they need not take any further action in order to lose weight. ERSP found that eating a low calorie dinner was a material condition to obtaining the claimed weight loss and must be prominently, clearly and conspicuously disclosed. ERSP also recommended that the marketer properly qualify the limitations of the applicability of consumer testimonials in future advertising.

Emson, Inc.
Ab Rocket Twister System
Case #268 (6.13.11)

Claim at Issue:

- *"Lose up to 2 inches off your waist in just 12 days guaranteed or your money back,"; "...in as little as 5 minutes a day with the Ab Rocket Twister, you're on your way to tighter, sexier abs guaranteed."; "I've lost over 50 pounds and 21 inches."*

ERSP Findings: ERSP determined that when certain versions of the Ab Rocket Twister advertising are viewed in their entirety, it would not be unreasonable for consumers to interpret the advertising as communicating that the stated results were based on use of the Ab Rocket Twister alone.

ERSP recommended that the marketer should modify such advertising to clearly communicate that the weight and inches lost depicted in the advertising were based upon adherence to all components of the Ab Rocket Twister System, not just use of the machine itself.

MZ Direct Response, LL&C
Velform Sauna Belt
Case #75 (2.21.06)

Claims at Issue:

- *Immediately see real results with no effort."*
- *"Lose an in inch in fifty minutes."*
- *"A safe sure way to lose weight."*
- *"We are able to target specific areas such as the abdomen, hips, and thighs."*

ERSP Findings: ERSP concluded that any performance claims characterized in an "instant" or "immediate" context that are inconsistent with results obtained after 50 minutes of product usage should be either adequately qualified or discontinued. ERSP also recommended that the marketer refrain from suggesting that consumers will lose meaningful (*i.e.,* "real results") weight with "*no effort.*" ERSP also determined that the marketer's claims to *"Lose an inch in 50 minutes"* as well as the on camera demonstrations of people losing more weight and inches in 50 minutes than reported by in the study should be discontinued or modified. Lastly, it was recommended that the marketer should also modify its computer-generated "slimdown" depiction to accurately reflect the evidence and not overstate the amount and areas of weight/inches loss that can be realized by use of the Velform Sauna Belt.

"Dr. Recommended" Claims

iSatori Technologies. LLC
Lean System 7
Case #4324 (4.22.05)

"Doctor Recommended" claims can carry great weight with consumers and, consequently, require strong evidence.

Claim at Issue:

• *Doctor Recommended*

NAD Findings: In addition to making unsupported "clinically proven" claims such as Lean System 7 will burn up to 930 extra calories a day, the advertiser also claimed that its product was "doctor recommended." In support of this claim, the advertiser submitted a testimonial from one doctor. NAD has recognized that "Doctor Recommended" claims can carry great weight with consumers and, consequently, require strong evidence. It is well-established that "doctor recommended" claims must be supported by well-conducted physician surveys based on doctors' actual experience in their daily practice. Here, the advertiser did not produce any evidence regarding its doctor recommended claim other than an unsupported testimonial from one doctor.

Senator MCCASKILL. Thank you.
Mr. Mister.

STATEMENT STEVEN M. MISTER, PRESIDENT AND CHIEF EXECUTIVE OFFICER, COUNCIL FOR RESPONSIBLE NUTRITION

Mr. MISTER. Good morning. My name is Steve Mister, and I'm the President and CEO of the Council for Responsible Nutrition.

CRN is the leading trade association representing the manufacturers and marketers of dietary supplements, functional foods, and their nutritional ingredients. We empathize with the many Americans who are vulnerable to false promises for losing weight fast, with everything from rubber pants and bracelets to sprays, creams and exercise gadgets, and, yes, dietary supplements. Collectively, Americans spend over $40 billion a year trying to lose weight. The Nutrition Business Journal reports that dietary supplements and meal replacements formulated for weight loss are a $5.3-billion-a-year industry, a small fraction of the total, but a significant sum nevertheless.

But, before the Committee throws the baby out with the bath water, we want to be clear that there are a number of dietary ingredients used in weight-loss supplements, when combined with moderate exercise programs and sensible eating, that have been shown in well-conducted clinical trials to be safe and beneficial for weight management. The Dietary Supplement Health and Education Act requires that all supplements must have substantiation for their claims, and that includes weight-loss claims.

The FDA's regulations for labeling establish a detailed approach for what constitutes adequate substantiation for these "structure/function" claims, which requires the claims be supported by well-conducted human trials with statistically significant benefits.

Along with the consumers who are duped by these false and misleading claims, the responsible supplement industry who complies with these standards also stands to lose when unscrupulous marketers take advantage with misleading and unsupported ads. I'm here today to reinforce the commitment of CRN's members to help address these scams and frauds in the weight-loss marketplace.

But, unfortunately, the reality of the current weight-loss market is that it is a tale of two industries: legitimate manufacturers who responsibly produce products that work and make claims for their products that are within the bounds of the law, and then, on the other hand, the unscrupulous players who prey on consumer desperation and their insatiable desire to be thin, and will say almost anything to make a quick profit.

The Federal Trade Commission has the authority to enforce the prohibition on false, misleading, and deceptive claims made in the advertising of weight-loss products. CRN has publicly supported, and will continue to applaud, the numerous enforcement actions brought by the FTC in recent years, and the more than $438 million in restitution and civil penalties assessed by the Commission against deceptive advertising with respect to weight-loss products since 2004.

Enforcement sweeps like the FTC's ''Operation Waistline'' and, more recently, ''Failed Resolution,'' and its media awareness campaigns like ''Gut Check,'' help to remove misleading claims, but they also alert the public while sending a message of deterrence through the industry. And CRN applauds them for that. However, the reality is that, in this Internet Age, along with a proliferation of cable television, talk radio, and various online media, and the increasing pressures for ad revenue among shrinking print media, both the FTC and the FDA have insufficient resources to combat the number of deceptive claims in the market. Some media outlets, eager to accept advertising dollars, will turn a blind eye to advertising copy that clearly violates the law and deceives consumers.

So, in 2006, CRN began an industrywide self-regulatory program with the National Advertising Division (NAD), as you've heard, to help self-police the advertising claims of dietary supplement marketers. CRN has committed over $2 million to underwrite this program, which has already investigated almost 200 challenges of the claims made by supplement marketers, many of which involve weight-loss claims. I am proud of the track record of this program for providing fair, thoughtful, and transparent decisions, for achieving a high rate of industry participation, and for the precedents that it sets with these decisions to deter others in the industry from making similarly fraudulent claims.

CRN's members are committed to manufacturing and marketing high-quality, safe, beneficial products and to ensure that our consumers receive truthful, accurate, nonmisleading information on supplements and nutritional products.

We believe the challenge for legitimate weight-loss products is essentially this: American consumers unrealistically yearn for a magic bullet, and unscrupulous marketers will take advantage of these desires with hollow promises. Like a successful weight-loss program, though, the solutions are not easy. Significant first steps should include: increasing resources and priorities for enforcement of the existing legal requirements by both the FTC and the FDA; expanding and strengthening self-policing programs among manufacturers and marketers in the industry, like our initiative with the NAD; calling on media outlets and online retailers to conduct their own advertising clearance before accepting ads with claims that are illegal and simply too good to be true; and finally, educating consumers to be realistic about their weight-loss strategies and their expectations, to make them less vulnerable to outrageous and unsupported claims.

Thank you for the opportunity to share our views with the Committee.

[The prepared statement of Mr. Mister follows:]

PREPARED STATEMENT OF STEVEN M. MISTER, PRESIDENT AND CHIEF EXECUTIVE OFFICER, COUNCIL FOR RESPONSIBLE NUTRITION

Good morning. My name is Steve Mister, and I am the President and CEO of the Council for Responsible Nutrition.

The Council for Responsible Nutrition (CRN) appreciates this opportunity to provide testimony to the Senate Subcommittee on Consumer Protection, Product Safety and Insurance. We want to reassure you and your colleagues, your constituents and our customers that CRN's members are committed to manufacturing and marketing high quality, safe and beneficial products that have a valuable and appropriate role in weight management regimens. CRN is also committed to ensuring that consumers receive truthful, accurate and non-misleading information about dietary supplements on the label and in advertising.

CRN, founded in 1973 and based in Washington, DC, is the leading trade association representing dietary supplement manufacturers and ingredient suppliers. CRN companies produce a large portion of the dietary supplements and nutritional products marketed in the United States and globally. Our member companies manufacture popular national brands as well as the store brands marketed by major supermarkets, drug stores and discount chains. These products also include those marketed through natural food stores and mainstream direct selling companies. CRN represents nearly 150 companies that manufacture or market dietary supplements, functional foods and their nutritional ingredients, or supply products and services to those suppliers and manufacturers. Our member companies comply with a host of Federal and state regulations governing dietary supplements in the areas of manufacturing, marketing, quality control and safety. Our supplier and manufacturer member companies also agree to adhere to additional voluntary guidelines as well as to CRN's Code of Ethics.

Weight management is a serious issue. According to the 2013 Gallup-Healthways Well-being Index, the number of adults in the U.S. who need to be more conscious of their weight continues to climb: 27 percent are classified as obese, and another 35 percent are considered overweight.[1] At the same time, a Gallup poll from last November indicates that 51 percent of Americans say they want to lose weight, but just under half of them—only 25 percent—say they are seriously trying to lose weight.[2]

So it's not surprising that these statistics translate into many Americans who are eager to drop a few pounds. We empathize with the many Americans who are vulnerable to false promises for losing weight fast with everything from rubber pants and bracelets, to sprays, creams, exercise gadgets and dietary supplements. Collectively, Americans spend about $40 billion a year trying to lose weight.[3] The Nutrition Business Journal reports that dietary supplements and meal replacements that are formulated for weight loss are a $5.3 billion industry[4] in the U.S., only a fraction of the total, but still a significant sum.

Now let's be clear: a number of dietary ingredients in weight loss supplements, when combined with moderate exercise programs and sensible eating, have been shown in well-regarded clinical trials to be safe and effective for weight management. The truth is that many dietary supplements, meal replacement programs and specially formulated foods can be beneficial as part of a weight management program. They can increase weight loss over diet and exercise alone, and can help people lead more active lifestyles that help to keep the pounds off.

At the same time, however, other products make outrageous claims that promise the weight will fall off without changing what you eat, and without exercise. Some products tout the latest "miracle" ingredients, falsely claim to be "clinically proven"

---

[1] U.S. Obesity Rate Climbing in 2013, Gallup, Nov. 1, 2013 *http://www.gallup.com/poll/165 671/obesity-rate-climbing-2013.aspx.*

[2] Americans' Desire to Shed Pounds Outweighs Effort, Gallup, Nov. 29, 2013, *http://www .gallup.com/poll/166082/americans-desire-shed-pounds-outweighs-effort.aspx.*

[3] Weight Management Trends in the U.S., 2nd ed. (March 15, 2013) *http://www.pack agedfacts.com/Weight-Management-Trends-7429799/.*

[4] Unpublished data from *Nutrition Business Journal,* provided June 12, 2014.

and may not even contain the levels of ingredients they promote. Some scammers trap consumers in fraudulent credit card programs or offer money-back guarantees but become impossible to track down when the product doesn't work. And that is the reality of the current weight loss market: it is a tale of two industries—with legitimate manufacturers who responsibly produce products that work and make claims for their products within the bounds of the law, and unscrupulous players who prey on desperation and the insatiable desire to be thin, and will say almost anything to make a quick profit. Along with consumers who are duped by false and misleading claims, the responsible supplement industry, who complies with these standards, also stands to lose when unscrupulous marketers take advantage with misleading and unsupported ads.

The Dietary Supplement Health and Education Act (''DSHEA'') requires that all supplements must have substantiation for the claims they make, and that includes weight loss claims. The Food and Drug Administration's (FDA) regulations establish detailed requirements for what constitutes adequate substantiation for these ''structure/function claims,'' which are modeled after Federal Trade Commission (FTC) standards for truthful and non-misleading advertising claims. These requirements can be found in the FDA's ''Guidance for Industry: Substantiation for Dietary Supplement Claims Made Under Section 403(r)(6) of the Federal Food, Drug and Cosmetic Act''[5] and its ''Guidance for Industry: Structure/Function Claims, Small Entity Compliance Guide.''[6] The generally accepted standards for the substantiation of weight management claims include requirements that there must be research on humans showing demonstrable weight loss; that the studies use the same ingredients at the same levels as contained in the products; and that the research shows a statistically significant benefit over placebo in double-blinded, placebo-controlled studies.

CRN is also greatly concerned about the ingredients found in some weight loss products that masquerade as dietary supplements for weight loss. Despite their labeling claims of being ''all natural'' and ''completely safe,'' some of these products contain prescription drug ingredients and are illegally and erroneously marketed as dietary supplements. FDA has taken enforcement actions with respect to no less than 250 products in the past six years. These products have contained ingredients like sibutramine, a powerful weight loss pharmaceutical ingredient that was removed from the market by FDA for safety reasons. These weight loss products are potentially dangerous to consumers because they may cause side effects or adverse interactions with other drugs, and because the product labeling fails to disclose the presence of these powerful substances, consumers are unaware of their presence. Although FDA has brought civil and criminal actions against some of the marketers of these illegal products, the agency must do more to protect consumers, including working more closely with the U.S. Justice Department to bring criminal charges against those who introduce these dangerous products into the market.

Just as DSHEA calls on FDA to oversee claims made in dietary supplement labeling, the Federal Trade Commission Act authorizes the FTC to enforce the prohibition on false, misleading and deceptive claims made in the advertising of weight loss products. The FTC's ''Dietary Supplements: An Advertising Guide for Industry''[7] describes in detail how the general principles of the statute apply specifically to the health-related claims made for dietary supplements, namely that advertising claims must be truthful, not misleading and substantiated with credible scientific evidence.

CRN has publicly supported—and will continue to applaud the numerous enforcement actions brought by the FTC in recent years and the more than $438 million in fines and penalties assessed by the Commission since 2004 against deceptive weight loss advertising. Enforcement sweeps like the FTC's ''Operation Waistline''[8] and its media awareness programs, like ''Gut Check: A Reference Guide for Media on Spotting False Weight Loss Claims,''[9] help to remove misleading advertising, and also alert consumers and send a message of deterrence throughout the industry.

For example, FTC's recently released ''Gut Check'' Guide offers tips for media to help identify weight loss claims that are likely to be too good to be true. It cautions media to review advertising before accepting it because certain claims from advertisers may be a tip-off to deception if the product claims to:

---

[5] *http://www.fda.gov/food/guidanceregulation/guidancedocumentsregulatoryinformation/ucm073200.htm.*

[6] *http://www.fda.gov/food/guidanceregulation/guidancedocumentsregulatoryinformation/ucm103340.htm.*

[7] *http://business.ftc.gov/documents/bus09-dietary-supplements-advertising-guide-industry.*

[8] *http://www.ftc.gov/news-events/press-releases/1997/03/ftc-announces-operation-waistline-law-enforcement-and-consumer.*

[9] *http://www.business.ftc.gov/documents/0492-gut-check-reference-guide-media-spotting-false-weight-loss-claims.*

1. cause weight loss of two pounds or more a week for a month or more without dieting or exercise;
2. cause substantial weight loss no matter what or how much the consumer eats;
3. cause permanent weight loss even after the consumer stops using the product;
4. block the absorption of fat or calories to enable consumers to lose substantial weight;
5. safely enables consumers to lose more than three pounds per week for more than four weeks;
6. cause substantial weight loss for all users; or
7. cause substantial weight loss by wearing a product on the body or rubbing it into the skin.

FTC also provides similar tips in its consumer information article "Weighing the Claims in Diet Ads," which warns consumers about ads promising quick and easy weight loss without diet or exercise and what claims are most likely to be untrue.

However, the reality is that in this Internet age, along with the proliferation of cable television, talk radio and various online media, and increasing pressures for shrinking ad revenue among print media, both the FTC and FDA have insufficient resources to combat the number of deceptive claims in the market. Some media outlets, eager to accept advertising dollars, turn a blind eye to advertising copy that clearly violates the law. Like the carnival game "whack-a-mole," it seems that every time the FTC targets one company for deceptive advertising, two more pop up. Responsible firms, like CRN's members, suffer along with consumers as legal, reasonable and defensible advertising for weight management gets dwarfed by outlandish claims that violate the law and deceive consumers.

In 2006, CRN began an industry program with the Council of Better Business Bureaus to help self-police the advertising claims of dietary supplement marketers. Over the past seven years, the National Advertising Division (NAD) has conducted almost 200 challenges of the claims made by supplement marketers, many of which involve weight loss. CRN has committed over $2 million to underwrite the program at the NAD devoted to the investigation of supplement claims. CRN is proud of the track record this program has for providing fair, thoughtful and transparent decisions, for achieving a high rate of participation with those decisions, and for the precedential effect these decisions have to deter others in the industry from making similarly fraudulent claims.

Almost 20 percent of all the cases the CRN-funded program with the NAD has considered involve claims for weight loss. Commonly recurring problems with these claims include promoting that the ingredients are "clinically proven" or "doctor recommended" when they are neither; claiming clinical research for a product when the study did not examine the same ingredients or ingredients at the same levels as they appear in the product, and test results that are wildly overstated in the advertising. While participation by the advertiser is voluntary, in cases where the advertiser refuses to participate, or where the NAD becomes aware that the advertiser fails to implement the changes recommended in the decision, those cases are referred to the FTC for review and possible legal action.

CRN has also developed a *Roadmap for Retailers,*[10] a six-page brochure to assist those who interact with our consumers, which reminds them that unsupported personal testimonials, promises of cures and treatments, and exaggerated claims that are not supported by the research are both illegal and detrimental to keeping the trust of their customers. CRN also provides "*A Dozen Tips for Consumers,*"[11] to help educate the public how to make savvy purchasing decisions. Separately, we have developed guidelines for the industry for the labeling of caffeine content in dietary supplements and functional foods, a common concern especially among weight loss products,[12] and we maintain a Code of Ethics for CRN members.[13]

CRN's members are committed to manufacturing and marketing high quality, safe and beneficial products. We are likewise committed to ensuring that consumers receive truthful, accurate and non-misleading information on dietary supplements. We believe that the challenge with weight loss products—whether they are dietary supplements, meal programs, clothing or gadgets—is that American consumers' unrealistic yearnings for a magic bullet align with the temptation for unscrupulous marketers to take advantage of these desires with hollow promises.

---

[10] *http://www.crnusa.org/roadmap/.*
[11] *http://www.crnusa.org/CRNfactsheetconsumertips.html*
[12] *http://www.crnusa.org/caffeine/guidelines.html.*
[13] *http://crnusa.org/wholssrlcode.html.*

Like a successful diet, the solutions are not simple or easy; however, we believe there are four significant steps that can be taken to help address these issues:

1. *Expanding and strengthening voluntary programs among manufacturers and marketers of weight loss products, like our initiative with the NAD.* These self-regulatory programs help consumers identify products that are likely to work and avoid those that aren't. Third-party certification programs that audit manufacturing practices and test ingredients against label claims can also help responsible marketers to distinguish their products from ones that don't measure up.

2. *Increasing resources and priorities for the enforcement of existing legal require- ments by both the FTC and FDA.* The legal standards for substantiation of claims made in product labeling and advertising, including Internet websites, are sufficient to protect consumers while balancing the rights of marketers to make truthful statements about their products and to present emerging science. However, more needs to be done to target bad actors and remove un- truthful claims. We urge Congress to provide adequate resources to both FDA and FTC with direction to the agencies to make prosecution of untruthful ad- vertising and labeling a priority.

3. *Calling on media outlets and online retailers to conduct their own advertising review before accepting advertising with claims that are illegal and simply ''too good to be true.''* Claims of dramatic weight loss that don't require any change in diet or exercise, that promise permanent fat reduction or that offer over- night results are inherently suspect. Media outlets, including newspapers, magazines, radio and television stations, Internet websites and social media sites, all have a role in helping to prevent consumer fraud. Incentives for these venues to screen advertising and reject ads that are blatantly deceptive must be strengthened.

4. *Educating consumers to be realistic about weight loss strategies and expectations to make them less vulnerable to outrageous and unsupported claims.* When consumers better understand that meaningful weight loss occurs slowly and steadily, and that so-called ''miracle'' products are non-existent, unscrupulous marketers will find less demand for their potions and gimmicks.

CRN shares this Committee's concerns about bad actors in the industry and we denounce false, misleading or deceptive marketing practices—activities engaged in by a few who have damaged the reputation of the responsible industry. We look forward to cooperating with the other witnesses at today's hearing to develop solutions that strengthen the trust of consumers in dietary supplements.

Thank you for the opportunity to share our views with the Committee.

Senator McCASKILL. Thank you, Mr. Mister.
Mr. Haralson.

STATEMENT OF ROBERT H. HARALSON IV, EXECUTIVE DIRECTOR, TRUSTINADS.ORG

Mr. HARALSON. Chairman McCaskill, Ranking Member Heller, and distinguished members of the Subcommittee, thank you for the opportunity to testify today about TrustInAd.org's member-companies' efforts to combat fraudulent online advertising for weight-loss products. My name is Rob Haralson, and I am the organization's Executive Director.

In my testimony, I will highlight how our member companies are incentivized to keep bad ads out of our systems. I will also note how they are investing significant resources in this area and have already removed millions of bad ads from their services.

TrustInAds.org includes Internet industry leaders AOL, Facebook, Google, Twitter, and Yahoo!. We founded this organization to work together toward a common goal: protect people from malicious online ads and deceptive practices. With this effort, we are bringing awareness to consumers about online ad-related scams, working collaboratively to identify both trends in deceptive ads and best practices, and sharing our knowledge with policy-makers and consumer advocates around the country.

TrustInAds.org offers guidance to consumers on how to avoid scams through the regular release of what we call our ''Bad Ads Trend Alerts.'' These are consumer-friendly and easily digestible reports that examine a specific trend or trends we are seeing, and provides specific examples of bad ads and websites that the companies have removed from their platforms. We highlight the steps that the companies have taken to combat the problem, and give the consumers useful tips on how to make good choices online. Our website also includes a dedicated page where people can go to learn how to easily report a suspicious ad on any of our member companies' websites.

Our first report, released in May, detailed ads for phony tech-support services. And yesterday, we released our newest report on fraudulent ads related to weight-loss products and dietary supplements. Our member companies have allocated significant resources to keep bad ads off their platforms. Without question, ensuring a positive user experience for all users is essential to maintaining a vibrant Internet ecosystem.

Today, the sale of numerous weight-loss products and dietary supplements through advertising is seen across all mediums: print, broadcast, radio, and the Web. And, while most entities selling these kinds of products provide accurate and truthful information regarding the overall effectiveness, some bad actors, in an attempt to entice consumers, market products with outrageous claims and promises of dramatic weight loss. For the bad actors attempting to use online advertising, these kinds of claims violate both our member companies' advertising policies and existing laws aimed at protecting consumers. We applaud Federal agencies for recognizing the weight-loss scam problem and their active efforts to educate consumers about misleading claims.

In addition to its active law enforcement against scammers, the FTC's Consumer Information Website has an entire section devoted to weight loss and fitness that outlines many of the advertisements that users could encounter on the Internet and other places, and debunks their claims. Stopping these ads is critical for online advertising companies, as well. Collectively, our member companies have hundreds of individuals on their respective teams, spanning policy, engineering, network security, and legal, that are dedicated to identifying and preventing this illegal activity.

Fortunately, most of these types of ads never reach the user and are immediately rejected through automated filtering processes as soon as they are submitted. For those that are detected after they are published, they are immediately removed, and the advertiser account is reviewed. Temporary or permanent suspension of the advertiser account is then considered, depending on the severity of the ad's policy violations.

User feedback also plays an important role in detecting bad ads, and our companies carefully review user complaints related to ads, and quickly take action when warranted.

Over the course of the past 18 months, AOL, Google, Facebook, Twitter, and Yahoo! have collectively removed or rejected over 2 and a half million ads related to weight loss and dietary supplements due to numerous ads policy violations.

While all stakeholders are working hard to stop these ads, weight-loss scammers, some who are incredibly sophisticated, work maliciously to find ways to avoid detection by agencies, falling within their guidelines, and circumvent our companies' automated filters. Working together, AOL, Facebook, Google, and Twitter, and Yahoo! are fully committed to improving their systems to help protect users across the Web. We believe that if we all work together to identify threats and stamp them out, we can make the Web a safer place for everyone.

Again, thank you for this opportunity to testify.

[The prepared statement of Mr. Haralson follows:]

PREPARED STATEMENT OF ROBERT H. HARALSON IV, EXECUTIVE DIRECTOR, TRUSTINADS.ORG

Chairwoman McCaskill, Ranking Member Heller and distinguished Members of the Subcommittee:

Thank you for the opportunity to testify today on TrustInAds.org's member companies' efforts to combat fraudulent online advertising for weight loss products. My name is Rob Haralson and I am the organization's Executive Director.

TrustInAds.org includes Internet industry leaders AOL, Facebook, Google, Twitter and Yahoo, and we founded this organization to work together toward a common goal: Protect people from malicious online advertisements and deceptive practices. With this effort, we are: bringing awareness to consumers about online ad-related scams and deceptive activities; collaborating to identify trends in deceptive ads and sharing best practices; and sharing our knowledge with policymakers and consumer advocates around the country.

TrustInAds.org offers guidance to consumers on how to avoid scams through the regular release of what we call our Bad Ads Trend Alerts. These are consumer-friendly and easily digestible reports that examine a specific trend or trends we are seeing, and provide specific examples of bad ads and websites the companies have removed from their platforms. We highlight steps the companies have taken to combat the problem and give consumers useful tips on how to make good consumer choices online.

In addition, our website includes a dedicated page where people can go to learn how to easily report a suspicious ad seen on any of our member companies' advertising platforms.

Our first report, released in May, detailed ads for phony tech support services, and yesterday, we released our newest report on fraudulent ads related to weight loss products and dietary supplements.

I have included this report as an attachment to my written testimony for the Subcommittee.

Our member companies are committed to protecting people from malicious online advertisements and deceptive practices and have allocated significant resources to keep these kinds of bad ads off of their platforms. Without question, ensuring a positive experience for all users is essential to maintaining a vibrant and successful Internet ecosystem.

Today, the sale of numerous weight loss products and dietary supplements through advertising is seen across all mediums—print, broadcast, radio and the web. And while most entities selling these kinds of products provide accurate and truthful information regarding their overall effectiveness, some bad actors—in an attempt to entice consumers—market products with outrageous, unrealistic claims and promises of dramatic weight loss.

For the bad actors attempting to use online advertising, these kinds of claims violate both TrustInAds.org's member companies' advertising policies and existing laws aimed at protecting consumers.

We applaud Federal agencies for recognizing the weight loss scam problem and their active efforts to educate consumers about misleading claims. In addition to its active law enforcement against scammers, the FTC's Consumer Information website has an entire section devoted to weight loss and fitness that outlines many of the advertisements that users could encounter on the Internet and debunks their claims. In addition, the Food and Drug Administration's (FDA) website brings regu-

52

latory actions against scammers and also provides consumers with helpful information about weight loss fraud.

Stopping these ads is critical for online advertising companies as well. Collectively, TrustInAds.org member companies have hundreds of individuals on their respective teams spanning policy, engineering, network security and legal dedicated to identifying and preventing this illegal activity.

Fortunately, most of these types of ads never reach the user and are immediately rejected through automated filtering processes as soon as they are submitted. For those that are detected after they are published, they are immediately removed and the advertiser account is reviewed. Temporary or permanent suspension of the advertiser account is then considered depending on the severity of the ads policy violation(s).

User feedback also plays an important role in detecting bad ads, and our companies carefully review user complaints related to ads and quickly take action when warranted.

Over the course of the past 18 months, AOL, Google, Facebook, Twitter and Yahoo have collectively removed or rejected over 2.5 million ads related to weight loss and dietary supplements due to numerous ads policy violations.

While all stakeholders are working hard to stop these ads, weight loss scammers, some who are incredibly sophisticated, work maliciously to find ways to avoid detection by agencies, falling within their guidelines, and circumvent our companies' automated filters. Given this, each company has allocated substantial technical, financial and human resources to stop bad advertising practices like these and protect users on their platforms and across the web.

The steps our member companies have taken aim to complement the continued efforts by agencies such as the FTC to enforce existing law to ensure that consumers are presented with truthful and accurate information in online ads.

Working together, AOL, Facebook, Google, Twitter and Yahoo are fully committed to improving their systems to help protect users across the web, contributing research, and facilitating industry initiatives to combat bad online ads. We believe that if we all work together to identify threats and stamp them out, we can make the web a safer place for everyone.

Again, thank you for this opportunity to testify.

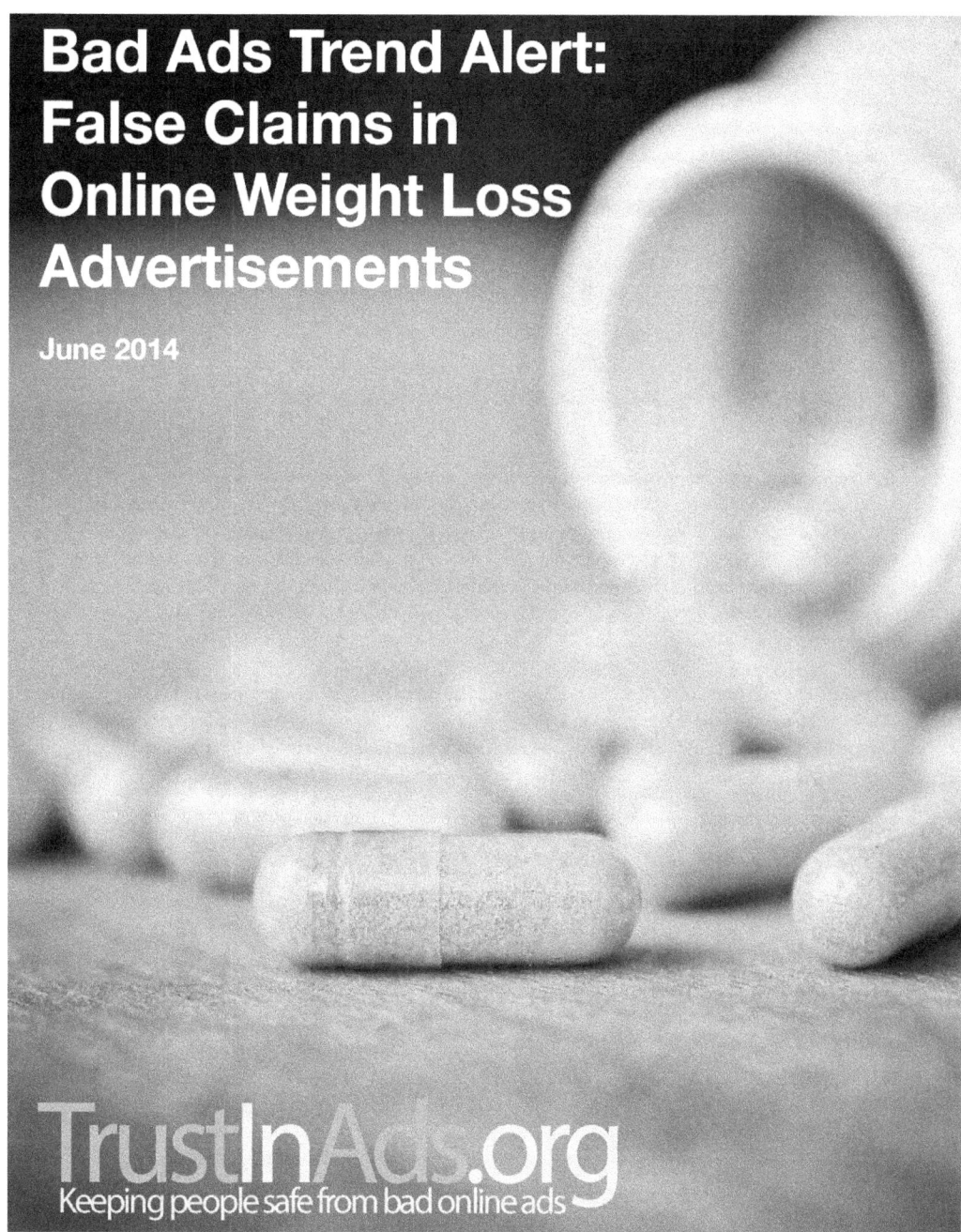

54

Today, the sale of numerous weight loss products and dietary supplements through advertising is seen across all mediums – print, broadcast, radio and the web. And while many entities selling these kinds of products provide accurate and truthful information regarding their overall effectiveness, some bad actors - in an attempt to entice consumers - market products with outrageous, unrealistic claims and promises of dramatic weight loss.

For the bad actors attempting to use online advertising, these kinds of claims violate the advertising policies of the companies that make up TrustInAds.org, in addition to laws aimed at protecting consumers.

Our member companies are committed to protecting people from malicious online advertisements and deceptive practices and have allocated significant resources to keep these kinds of bad ads off of their platforms.

The steps our member companies have taken aim to complement the many ongoing efforts by agencies to enforce existing law to ensure that consumers are presented with truthful and accurate information in online ads. For example, the Federal Trade Commission (FTC) has a long, continuing history of bringing law enforcement matters to stop deceptive weight loss advertising, as well as providing education to consumers and media companies about avoiding these ads. Similarly, the Food and Drug Administration (FDA) brings regulatory actions against deceptive advertisers, in addition to consumer education.

Challenges remain in the ability for online advertising platforms to effectively determine the validity of some of the claims made by websites selling these products. However, TrustInAds.org member companies are working diligently to combat scammers and are committed to working with all stakeholders to determine the best and most effective ways to keep bad ads of the web.

INTRODUCTION

The websites often look enticing - "Lose 30 pounds in 30 days!" or some other similar claim serves as the focal point of the page. "Burn Fat Without Diet or Exercise!" and "Boost Your Metabolism!" are other catchphrases used to encourage the visitor to click the "Order Now" button. These sites are selling dietary supplements like Acai Berry, Raspberry Ketone, and Garcinia Cambogia using outlandish and false claims of miracle methods to dramatically shed pounds instantly. They often attempt to further legitimize their products with fake reviews and endorsements from reputable sources like celebrities or mainstream media outlets.

The entities operating these websites use a number of marketing tactics to promote these products to consumers, including attempts to serve online ads on AOL, Facebook, Google, Twitter, Yahoo, and other online advertising platforms. TrustInAds.org's member companies all have advertising policies in place for health and wellness-related advertisements and work hard to prevent ads that promote false claims from ever reaching the user through tools like automated filters. Advertisers are required to strictly adhere to these policies. However, sophisticated scammers work maliciously to circumvent companies' automated filters and sometimes a small number of these ads do end up on the web.

Our companies have strong incentives to keep these and other bad ads off of the internet and are committed to working with the FTC in their efforts to protect consumers. As we have stated publicly before, ensuring a positive experience for all users is essential to maintaining a vibrant and successful internet ecosystem.

In this Trend Alert, TrustInAds.org examines these kinds of scam ads, highlights specific examples of ads and websites that our member companies have encountered and removed from their platforms, and provides basic tips for consumers to stay safe and make good consumer choices online.

ONLINE WEIGHT LOSS ADS AND WEBSITES

Below are examples of ads (Fig. 1) and websites (Fig. 2) that, after review, were disabled from of TrustInAds.org member companies' platforms.

Fig. 1 - Advertisements

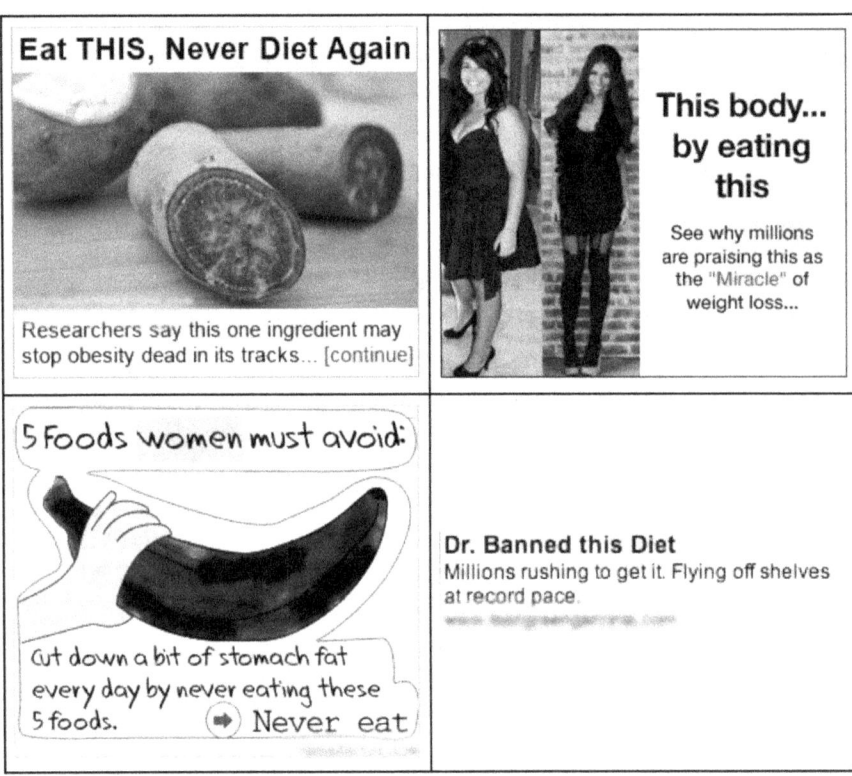

Fig. 2 - Websites

For these types of ads and websites (and the related advertiser accounts), the most common patterns that were detected by TrustInAds.org member companies and found to be in violation of advertising policies included:

- Outrageous or misleading claims in the ad or on the website landing page
- Websites with fake reviews or perceived endorsements from reputable sources
- Fake news or consumer alert websites that purport to be objective articles approving of the piece
- Hidden or recurring billing schemes that were misleading to the user

FEDERAL EFFORTS AND ACTIONS AGAINST DIET SCAMMERS

We applaud federal agencies for recognizing the weight loss scam problem and their active efforts to educate consumers about misleading claims. For example, the FTC's Consumer Information website has an entire section devoted to weight loss and fitness that outlines many of the advertisements that users could encounter on the internet and debunks their claims. The FDA's website also provides consumers with helpful information about weight loss fraud.

These agencies allow users to report deceptive weight loss ads, provide tips for consumers on how to lead an active, healthy lifestyle and directs them to several free, online resources to learn more about effective ways to lose weight.

In addition to providing consumers with resource pages, the agencies are continually policing the space as well. For example, the FTC recently announced that it filed suit against a Florida-based company behind Pure Green Coffee for using fake weight loss claims and fabricated news stories, which included logos of major news outlets, to advertise its dietary supplement. The FDA also brings regulatory actions, and frequently sends companies warning letters to stop deceptive weight loss claims.

Both agencies also provide guidance to industry. One recent effort that deserves special note is the FTC's extensive guidance for media companies to avoid running these deceptive ads. In its "Gut Check: A Reference Guide for Media on Spotting False Weight Loss Claims," the FTC outlines seven common false claims found in weight loss ads that should immediately raise red flags for publishers. This "Gut Check" provides important information for companies to catch the "worst-of-the-worst" ads, as well as critical guidance for the manual review of advertisements.

ACTIONS TAKEN BY OUR MEMBER COMPANIES

Of course, media companies must also take responsibility to protect their consumers. Because these deceptive advertisers use online ads, TrustInAds.org's member companies all have advertising policies in place that prohibit misleading health and wellness-related advertisements. Advertisers are clearly required to strictly adhere to these policies.

In addition, TrustInAds.org's member companies work hard to enforce these policies to prevent ads that promote false claims from ever reaching the users. All of our member companies have allocated substantial technical, financial and human resources to stop bad advertising practices and protect users on their platforms and across the web. Collectively, TrustInAds.org member companies have several hundred individuals spanning policy, engineering, information security, and legal fields dedicated to identifying, investigating, and preventing this abusive activity.

Fortunately, most of these types of ads never reach the user and are immediately rejected through automated filtering processes as soon as they are submitted. For those that are detected after they are published, they are immediately removed and the advertiser account is reviewed. Temporary or permanent suspension of the advertiser account is then considered depending on the severity of the ads policy violation(s).

However, sophisticated scammers are always attempting to circumvent companies' automated filters and sometimes a small number of these ads do end up on the web. The issue - as a whole - is incredibly nuanced and scammers frequently find new ways to avoid detection by companies and law enforcement, as well as working around the FTC guidelines. This makes it extremely difficult for online advertising platforms to identify scam ads among the billions of legitimate ads served every year. For example:

- The guidelines recommend that publishers should be wary of ads that claim their product causes "substantial" weight loss. However, the subjectivity of the term "substantial" creates a grey area through which publishers must maneuver. Many of these bad actors are experts at walking a fine line to make their ads appear acceptable within the guidelines, especially to automated filtering technology or other methods to scan ads at scale.

- The FTC has made clear that advertisers cannot misleadingly claim that their products' results are "backed by scientific research" or "clinical studies". However, assessing the validity of these reports for the thousands of websites that are advertised is an undertaking for which online advertising platforms are not equipped to manage, at least at scale. Many of the dietary supplements that are advertised through these ads are not subject to FDA approval, so the information needed to confirm these claims is not readily available.

Our member companies also rely on human review and analysis once specific ads or trends are recognized as potentially problematic from a variety of sources. For example, feedback from consumers and press releases from agencies play important roles in detecting bad ads, and our companies carefully review feedback related to ads and quickly take action when warranted. In addition, our member companies' dedicated teams are always on the lookout themselves for the latest trends.

Over the course of the past 18 months, AOL, Google, Facebook, Twitter and Yahoo have collectively removed or rejected over 2.5 million ads related to weight loss and dietary supplements due to numerous ads policy violations.

Our companies have strong incentives to keep these and other bad ads off of the internet and are working to establish more effective ways to collaborate with agencies in their efforts to protect consumers. As we have stated publicly before, ensuring a positive experience for all users is essential to maintaining a vibrant and successful internet ecosystem.

TIPS TO STAY SAFE

The phrase "if it sounds too good to be true, it probably is" certainly rings true with dietary supplement and weight loss advertisements and websites. TrustInAds.org encourages consumers to make careful considerations when purchasing any of these kinds of products.

- **Know the facts**. For any dietary supplement or weight loss product, always consult with your physician on the best course of action.

- **Watch out for these common themes**. On its website, the FTC provides a helpful list of common claims made by scammers selling these kinds of products, like:

  - "Lose weight without diet or exercise!"
  - "Lose weight no matter how much you eat of your favorite foods!"
  - "Lose weight permanently! Never diet again!"
  - "Lose 30 pounds in 30 days!"

  In addition, scammers also set up fake news sites using logos of legitimate news organizations to falsely promote endorsements of their products.

- **There simply are no magic pills, patches or creams**. Unfortunately, science has not produced a pill that we can simply take to help us shed the pounds without diet or exercise. Always be suspicious of these kinds of claims.

- **If you see a suspicious advertisement on our platforms, REPORT IT!** As we highlighted in our last report, one of the best ways we can defend users from harmful scams and bad ads is through user feedback. Each of the TrustInAds.org member companies have simple ways to alert them of potential scams and bad ads. Visit http://TrustInAds.org/report to learn how.

In addition, consumers are encouraged to report potential bad ads on the Federal Trade Commission's website at http://ftc.gov/complaint.

ABOUT TRUSTINADS.ORG

TrustInAds.org comprises a group of internet industry leaders that have come together to work toward a common goal: Protect people from malicious online advertisements and deceptive practices. With this effort, TrustInAds.org and its member companies are: Bringing awareness to consumers about online ad-related scams and deceptive activities; collaborating to identify trends in deceptive ads and sharing best practices; and sharing our knowledge with policymakers and consumer advocates around the country. To learn more, visit http://trustinads.org.

Follow us on Twitter @trustinads, Facebook http://facebook.com/trustinads and Google+.

Senator McCASKILL. Thank you, Mr. Haralson. Dr. Fabricant.

STATEMENT OF DANIEL FABRICANT, Ph.D., CHIEF EXECUTIVE OFFICER AND EXECUTIVE DIRECTOR, NATURAL PRODUCTS ASSOCIATION

Dr. FABRICANT. Thank you. Thank you, Madam Chair, members of the Committee. Thank you for this opportunity to discuss and participate in this panel discussion.

I am Dr. Daniel Fabricant, CEO and Executive Director of the National Products Association, the oldest and largest trade association in the natural products industry. We represent thousands of retailers, manufacturers, suppliers, and distributors of health foods, dietary supplements, natural personal care, and the millions of Americans who use supplements each year. While some of our members are household names, most are small-business owners, many women-owned, who got into this business because they want to help people live truly healthier lives.

Our first rule to customers is: Always consult with your healthcare provider and that dietary supplements are part of a broader, healthier lifestyle that includes diet and exercise.

Madam Chair, our members fully support efforts to combat fraud and to rules and regulations the Federal Government has to protect consumers. Deceptive advertising is illegal and should not be tolerated, period.

Like you, we are especially concerned about fraud on the Internet. Our association was founded by brick-and-mortar independent retailers, not Internet-only or fly-by-night firms. Our members know that public trust with their customer is one of the main reasons that natural products are in such high demand.

No one has more of an interest in weeding out fraud than our members, because bad actors only tarnish their good integrity. To support FTC, NPA has its own industry policing program, where members report questionable ad claims so bad actors can be disciplined. Our members are empowered to follow the Homeland Security rule as it relates to questionable ad claims: If you see something, say something.

Under our Truth in Advertising Program, questionable ad claims are reviewed by a committee of industry attorneys to determine if they are over the line, and then we take two actions. The first is to mail a cease and desist letter to a company. I've attached an example of that in my testimony. The second is to refer cases to FTC and FDA, where potentially fraudulent advertising or disease claims exist. Since this program began, in 2010, it has resulted in 446 letters to such firms. Of those, 320 acknowledged the issues and made corrections. The remainder were submitted to FDA and FTC over that period of time. So, we do have a strong partnership with the regulatory agencies, but we do depend on Federal authorities to provide enforcement action and make all of this a reality.

And here, while we see positive action, we also see some areas for consideration and some areas of concern. We've heard about existing enforcement authorities, but some are finally very used— being used for the first time. My former job was as director of Dietary Supplement Programs at FDA, where we used existing tools, like mandatory recall, administrative detention, injunctions and seizures, for firms—recidivist firms failing to meet minimal quality standards in making disease claims. FTC has, likewise, taken substantial actions against firms that have deceived consumers with regards to weight loss.

NPA fully supports those efforts, as they demonstrate FTC's ample and adequate current authorities, but we're still wrestling with the Internet advertising today and the fly-by-night issues, so where are we there with those? We believe FTC should consider using existing authorities more on the front end, to be more agile and disciplinary to companies without regard to their revenues. More aggressive enforcement of the so-called fly-by-nights needs to be just as important to the FTC as large-scale enforcement against larger revenue firms. FTC, in conjunction with Department of Justice and other agencies, currently use misdemeanor prosecutions, set civil money penalties for those already under consent orders or those who have violated other laws. However, we don't see as much use of these tools. Also, it appears there's a predilection by regulators to pursue more sizable and protracted cases, perhaps at the expense of more regulatory muscle on the front end against companies of any size or revenue stream. If FTC doesn't act and take down fly-by-nights on the front end early in the game, more will be tempted to get into the game.

Last, when we support the FTC's mission, we're concerned with a recent development related to FTC consent orders. Obviously, consent orders are case-specific and not meant to be applied industrywide. However, we are seeing some evidence of this, which could have negative outcomes for consumers, from both a cost perspective but also potentially reducing the quality and quantity of information about the products available to them.

When application of extrastatutory interpretations moves from consent orders into rules of general applicability, it's not beneficial to anyone, and particularly to consumers. One example would be FTC's new requirement—apparent new requirement that additional studies and research are necessary prior to advertising, like a requirement to conduct two double-blind randomized control studies to support lawful structure function statements, which is not a current legal or statutory requirement. This is not only outside of the statute, but leads to unnecessary and inefficient use of resources, which can chill innovation and disincentivizes the very research needed to substantiate claims.

This is also happening without any cost benefit on behalf of consumers or the economy. If such standards are applied generally, a firm investing in the currently required study that is well controlled and meets both the competent and reliable scientific standard would be prohibited from sharing that information from consumers. This actually results in less information being available to consumers, not more, and effectively changes the rules in the middle of the game. This is a critical concern to our members, as it appears to abridge protected speech, which could constitute a violation of APA or present possible First Amendment issues.

We'd like to work with FTC and others to address these concerns and to help improve the enforcement regime, and ultimately protect consumers while giving them the widest access to the information that they need.

Madam Chair, thank you for holding this hearing.

[The prepared statement of Dr. Fabricant follows:]

PREPARED STATEMENT OF DANIEL FABRICANT, PH.D., CHIEF EXECUTIVE OFFICER AND EXECUTIVE DIRECTOR, NATURAL PRODUCTS ASSOCIATION

Madam Chairperson and Members of the Committee;

Thank you for the opportunity to participate in this very important panel discussion. I am Dr. Daniel Fabricant, the CEO and Executive Director of the Natural Products Association (NPA). NPA is a 78-year old association and is the oldest and largest trade association in the natural products industry. We represent the interests of more than 10,000 locations, including retailers, manufacturers, suppliers and distributors of health foods, dietary supplements, natural personal care and the millions of Americans who use supplements each year.

While some of our members are household names, the majority of our members are small business owners—many women-owned—who got into this business because they want to help people live healthier lives through the use of natural products. And Americans are looking more and more for natural products each and every day, because they see the difference natural products can make in their daily lives. In 2012, Americans spent $2.8 trillion on health care, including $267 billion on health-related products and services, like dietary supplements, weight-loss programs and fitness club memberships. Our first rule to all customers is to always consult with your health care provider, and that dietary supplements are part of a broader healthy lifestyle that includes diet and exercise.

Madam Chair, let me say at the outset that our members fully support efforts to combat fraud and to enforce the range of rules and regulations that the Federal Government has to protect consumers and to give them the information they need. Deceptive advertising is illegal and should not be tolerated, period.

Advertising for weight loss covers a broad jurisdiction that spans a growing range of the economy, from exercise regimens, to meal systems, to cosmetic/spa type services and also includes a sector of the natural products industry in the form of dietary supplements.

At the NPA, we share the concerns expressed by others at this hearing about the use of deceptive advertising, especially on the internet. Our association was founded by brick-and-mortar independent retailers, not Internet only, fly-by night outfits. Our members know that the public trust with their customers is one of the main reasons that natural products are so prevalent in the marketplace these days.

In short, no one has more of an interest in weeding out fraud than our members, because bad actors only tarnish their good integrity. That's why we strongly support the Federal Trade Commission's (FTC) efforts.

To support FTC further, NPA has its own industry policing program where members identify and report questionable ad claims so that bad actors can be disciplined by Federal authorities, including the FTC. In short, our members are empowered to follow the homeland security rule as it relates to questionable ad claims: if you see something, say something.

NPA's educational foundation, The Natural Products Foundation (NPF) manages our Truth in Advertising (TIA) program. NPA members report questionable ad claims to an internal TIA committee of legal counsel. This special committee reviews claims to determine if they are over the line and then takes two actions.

The first is to mail a cease and desist letter to a company it deems has crossed that line. I have an example of that letter here that I will attach to my testimony. The second is to refer cases to FTC and FDA where potentially fraudulent advertising persists.

Since the truth in advertising program has begun, The TIA program has issued a total of 446 of these letters to companies. Of those, 320 acknowledged the issues noted and made immediate changes. If companies do not take immediate action, the TIA committee refers them directly to FTC and FDA. Our TIA group also meets regularly with officials at each agency to help identify and weed out fraud.

Our TIA program shows that NPA members want those who don't play by the rules brought into compliance or pushed out of any appearance of being a part of the legitimate industry that so many Americans look to for their health and wellness.

So we view our role as playing a strong partnership with regulatory officials, since we share their goals and objectives. But we do depend on Federal authorities to provide that enforcement action to make all of this a reality. In this arena, we see positive action, as well as some areas for consideration and some of concern.

As we have heard this morning, the dietary supplement industry is regulated both by the FTC as well as the Food and Drug Administration (FDA), where I served previously as the Director of Dietary Supplement Programs. FDA can take a substantial number of enforcement actions, and in the recent past has used some for the first time: including mandatory recall, administrative detention, and injunctions and seizures for those recidivist firms failing to meet minimal quality standards. As we heard earlier, under a Memorandum of Understanding (MOU) with the FDA, the FTC has primary regulatory responsibility with respect to the truth or falsity of all advertising (other than labeling) of foods, devices, cosmetics, and weight loss services. Under those current authorities, the FTC has taken substantial action against firms that have deceived consumers with regards to weight loss.

NPA fully supports those efforts, as they demonstrate FTC's ample and adequate current authority to enforce against deceptive advertising practices and protect consumers against fraud. But as helpful a deterrent as these high-profile cases are, we still wrestle with the Internet advertising and fly-by-night issues we are discussing today, so what to do about that?

We believe one area for consideration would be to encourage FTC to use existing authorities more on the front end: to be more agile and disciplinary to companies without regard to revenues. In other words, we think that more aggressive enforcement of the Internet fly-by-nights needs to be just as important a priority for FTC as the large-scale enforcement actions which we also support.

For example, FTC currently has as part of its enforcement arsenal very effective tools like misdemeanor prosecutions and civil monetary penalties which it uses very well for those already under consent orders or who have violated other applicable laws. But in our view, it appears that there is a predilection by regulators to pursue these more sizable and protracted cases, perhaps at the expense of more regulatory muscle on the front end against companies of any size or revenue stream.

A more balanced approach would both help curb the deceptive advertising and also serve as a helpful deterrent for other bad actors who might think they can get away with it. If FTC doesn't take down any fly-by-nights, more will unfortunately be tempted to get into the game.

Lastly, while we support the FTC's mission to prevent and punish unfair and deceptive acts, we are concerned with a recent development as it pertains to the use of FTC consent orders, which may have unintended consequences for consumers. Obviously, consent orders are case specific: they are not designed to be applied across the industry. However, we are seeing some evidence that this is happening, which we believe could have negative outcomes for consumers both from a cost perspective, but also in potentially *reducing* the quality and quantity of information about products available to them.

When application of extra-statutory interpretations moves from consent orders into rules of general applicability, such overreach is not beneficial to anyone and particularly to consumers. One example would be FTC's apparent new requirement that additional studies and research are necessary prior to advertising. Specifically, I'm referring to a requirement to conduct two double-blind, randomized control trials to support legal structure/function statements, which is not a current legal or regulatory requirement.

This is not only outside of the statute, but leads to unnecessary and inefficient use of resources, which chills innovation and dis-incentivizes the very research needed to substantiate claims (in an environment where recouping research dollars on natural products is very difficult because of the way the patent rules govern our industry, but that's a subject for another hearing).

Moreover, this is being done without any cost-benefit analysis on behalf of consumers or the economy. For example, if such standards are applied generally, a firm investing in the currently-required study that is well controlled and meets both the competent and reliable scientific standards would be prohibited from sharing those findings with consumers. It would actually result in less information being available to consumers—not more—and effectively changes the rules in the middle of the game. This is a critical concern, as it appears to abridge protected speech, which could constitute a violation of the Administrative Procedure Act (APA) or present possible first amendment issues.

We would like to work with FTC and others to address these concerns, to help improve the enforcement regime and ultimately to protect consumers while giving them the widest access to the information they need.

Madam Chair, thank you for holding his hearing. We support efforts to stop illegal consumer fraud. We strongly support resources for government agencies to enforce the law, in addition to any discussion on how current programs can be aligned across agencies to better protect consumers.

We stand ready to work with the Committee, the government, NGO's and supporting agencies to help identify and remove criminal activity which is the root cause of this matter, from the system.

Thank you and I look forward to your questions.

Senator MCCASKILL. Great. Thank you.

We'll have questions. And we have votes that begin in a little less than an hour, so hopefully we'll have an opportunity, everyone who is here, to have at least two rounds of questions.

I can't figure this out, Dr. Oz. I get that you do a lot of good on your show. I understand that you give a lot of great information about health, and you do it in a way that's easily understandable. You're very talented. You're obviously very bright. You've been trained in science-based medicine.

Now, here are three statements you made on your show. "You may think magic is make-believe, but this little bean has scientists saying they've found the magic weight-loss cure for every body type. It's green coffee extract." "I've got the number one miracle in a bottle to burn your fat. It's Raspberry Ketone." "Garcinia Cambogia. It may be the simple solution you've been looking for to bust your body fat for good."

I don't get why you need to say this stuff, because you know it's not true. So, why, when you have this amazing megaphone and this amazing ability to communicate, why would you cheapen your show by saying things like that?

Dr. OZ. Well, if I could disagree about whether they work or not, and I'll move on to the issue of the words that I used. And just with regard to whether they work or not, take the green coffee bean extract, as an example. I'm not going to argue that it would FDA-muster if it was a pharmaceutical drug seeking approval, but among the natural products that are out there, this is a product that has several clinical trials. There was one large one, a very good-quality one, that was done the year we talked about this, in 2012. Listen, I give——

Senator MCCASKILL. No, what I want to know—I want to know about that clinical trial, because the only one I know is 16 people in India that was paid for by the company. In fact, at the point in time you initially talked about this being a miracle, the only study that was out there was the one with 16 people in India that was written up by somebody who was being paid by the company that was producing it.

Dr. Oz. Well, this paper argued that there was no one paying for it, but I have the four papers—five papers, actually—plus a series of basic science papers on it, as well.

But, Senator McCaskill, if I—we can spend a lot of time arguing the merits of whether green coffee bean extract is worth trying or not worth trying. Many of the things that we argue that you do with regard to your diet are likewise criticizable. I mean, should you be on a low-fat diet, a low-carb diet? We'd be—I've spent a good part of my career recommending that folks have a low-fat diet. We've come full circle on that argument now, and no longer recommend that, many of us who practice medicine, because we realized that it wasn't working for our patients.

So, it is remarkably complex, as you know, to figure out what works for most people, even, in a dietary program. Even in the practice of medicine, we evolve by looking at new ideas, challenging orthodoxy, and evolving them.

So, when I hold—you know, these are the five papers. These are clinical papers. And we can argue about the quality of them, very justifiably. I can pick part papers that showed no benefit, as well. But, at the end of the day, if I have clinical subjects, real people having undergone trials—and, in this case, I actually gave it to members of my audience. It wasn't a formal trial, it was just an—
—

Senator McCaskill. Which wouldn't pass the—the trial you did with your audience, you would not——

Dr. Oz. No, of course not.

Senator McCaskill.—say that would ever pass scientific muster.

Dr. Oz. No, I would never publish the paper. It wasn't done under the appropriation IRB guidance. That wasn't the purpose of it. The purpose was for me to get a thumbnail sketch, Was this worth talking to people about, or not? But, again, I don't think this ought to be a referendum on the use of alternative medical therapies, because, if that's the case—listen, I've been criticized for having folks come on my show talking about the power of prayer. Now, again, as a practitioner, I can't prove that prayer helps people survive an illness. I know they had as——

Senator McCaskill. But, you don't have to buy prayer, Dr. Oz.

Dr. Oz. It's hard to buy prayer. That's the difference.

Senator McCaskill. Prayer is free.

Dr. Oz. Yes, prayer is free. And people—that's a very good point. [Laughter.]

Dr. Oz. Thankfully, prayer is free. And so, when—but, I see, in the hospital, when folks are feeling discomfort in their life—and a lot of it's emotional—when they have people praying for them, it lightens their burden.

So, my show was about hope. I wanted—and, as you very kindly stated, we've engaged millions of people in programs, including programs we did with the CDC, to get folks to realize that there are different ways that they get to rethink their future, that their best years aren't behind them, they're in front of them, and they actually can lose weight.

So, if I can just get across the big message that I actually do personally believe in the items that I talk about on the show. I passionately study them. I recognize that oftentimes they don't have the scientific muster to present as fact, but, nevertheless, I would give my audience the advice I give my family all the time—and I have given my family these products, specifically the ones you mentioned—then I—I'm comfortable with that part.

The—where I do think I've made it more difficult for the FTC is that, in an intent to engage viewers, I used flowery language, I used language that was very passionate, but it ended up not being helpful, but incendiary. And it provided fodder for unscrupulous advertisers.

And so, that clip that you played, which is over 2 years old—and I've done hundreds of segments since then—we have specifically restricted our use of words. We—literally not speaking about things I would otherwise talk about. There's a product that I've never talked about in the show that I feel very strongly about, because I know what will happen. I will say something very—in fact, we did a show with Yakon syrup, which you did not bring up. It was a—it is a South American root that had a big study published on it—I think, a very high-quality study—where they showed, not only did it help people lose weight, but, more importantly, helped their health. It was done on women who were diabetic. Done by an academic center down there. It was not funded by industry. And we talked about it, and I used as careful language as I could. And still there were Internet scam ads picking one or two supportive words, where of course I support them—I wouldn't be talking about it, otherwise——

Senator MCCASKILL. Well——

Dr. Oz.—and they still ended up out there.

Senator MCCASKILL.—listen, I'm surprised that you are defending—I mean, I've tried to really do a lot of research in preparation for this hearing, and the scientific community is almost monolithic against you, in terms of the efficacy of the three products that you called miracles. And when you call a product a miracle, and it's something you can buy, and it's something that gives people false hope—I just don't understand why you needed to go there. You've got so much you do on your show that makes it different and controversial enough that you get lots of views. I understand you're in a business of getting viewers, but I would ask you to look at the seven claims that the FTC put out on the Gut Check. It's very simple. "Causes weight loss of 2 pounds or more a week for a month without dieting or exercise; causes substantial weight loss, no matter how much you eat; causes permanent weight loss," like you said, "looking for to bust your body fat for good." If you just look at those seven, and if you spend time on your show telling people that these are the seven things you should know, that there isn't magic in a bottle, that there isn't a magic pill, that there isn't some kind of magic root or acai berry or Raspberry Ketone that's going to all of a sudden make it not matter that you're not moving and eating a lot of sugar and carbohydrates. I mean, do you disagree with any of these seven?

Dr. Oz. Senator McCaskill, I know the seven. I say those things on my show all the time. When I——

Senator MCCASKILL. Well, then why would you say that something is a miracle in a bottle?

Dr. Oz. My job, I feel, on the show is to be a cheerleader for the audience. And when they don't think they have hope, when they don't think they can make it happen, I want to look, and I do look, everywhere, including in alternative healing traditions, for any evidence that might be supportive to them. So, you pick on green coffee bean extract. With the amount of information that I have on that, I still am comfortable telling folks that, if you can buy a reputable version of it—and I say this all the time—I don't sell it, and these are not for long-term use—and by the way, with green coffee bean extract as an example, it's 1 pound a week over the duration of the different trials that have been done. That happened to be the same amount of weight that was lost by the 100 or so folks on the show who came on. And half of them got a placebo. We actually got fake pills, gave it to half the people, real pills to the other half. And it's sort of the same thumbnail. I'm looking at—a rough idea—if you can lose a pound a week more than you would have lost, doing the things you should be doing already—you can't sprinkle it on kielbasa and expect it to work. But, if that trial data is what's mimicked in your life, and you get a few pounds off, it jumpstarts you and gives you confidence to keep going, and then you start to follow the things that we talk about every single day, including all those seven items. I think it makes sense.

Senator MCCASKILL. Well, I'm going to give time to my colleagues now, and hopefully I'll have a chance to visit with some of the other witnesses in the next round. I will just tell you that— I know you feel that you're a victim, but sometimes conduct invites being a victim. And I think if you would be more careful, maybe you wouldn't be victimized quite as frequently.

Dr. Oz. Senator McCaskill, it—those topics you mentioned are over 2 years old. I have not been talking about products in that way for 2 years. And it has not changed at all what I'm seeing on the Internet. And, frankly, it's getting worse. So, I completely heed your commentary, and I realize—to my colleagues at the FTC— that I have made their jobs more difficult. That's why I came today.

Senator MCCASKILL. Good.

Dr. Oz. I'm cheerleading for this process. I want to do anything I can to help, but taking away those words doesn't change the problem that's already happened.

Senator MCCASKILL. Senator Heller.

Senator HELLER. Thank you.

You're the popular person, I guess, on the witness stand today, Dr. Oz.

[Laughter.]

Senator HELLER. And I just had a group of students, outside, and they all knew who you were. So, I asked these students, who— clearly, their parents or someone watch your show and pay attention.

Let me ask—let's be real clear. Do you believe that there's a miracle pill out there?

Dr. Oz. There's not a pill that's going to help you, long term, lose weight and live your—the best life without diet and exercise.

Senator HELLER. Do you believe there's a magic weight-loss cure out there?

Dr. Oz. It—the word—if you're selling something because it's magical, no. If you're arguing that it's going to be like magic, because if you stop eating carbohydrates, you're going to lose a lot of weight, that's a truthful statement. You may not agree with the flowery use of the word ''magic,'' but it is true that most people cutting out simple carbs will lose weight.

Senator HELLER. Well, tell me what works for most people. You mentioned that to the Chairman. What works for most people?

Dr. Oz. What works for most people is a diet based on real food, food that comes out of the ground looking the way it looks when you eat it, that's not been processed, with some physical activity. Most of weight loss, I believe, is about the food choices you make. Most are—keeping your weight low is about the physical activity you engage in.

Senator HELLER. OK. And it is true that you do not endorse any products or receive any money from any product sold?

Dr. Oz. That is true.

Senator HELLER. OK. Now, you've worked—you said you had some ideas, because you've worked to stop advertisers from using your names and likeness. And, in your testimony, you address online advertisements. What would you like to see done?

Dr. Oz. If I can just give three ideas. I'm just trying to be constructive.

Senator HELLER. I'd like to hear them.

Dr. Oz. I think the private sector can help by creating a Quick Reference Registry that lists celebrities who are legitimately connected to products. So, I don't happen to have any products that I sell, but whether the services are being promised—Ellen Degeneres, Jimmy Fallon, Rachael Ray, and the list of scam celebrities goes on—if all of us made a list of what products we actually do work with, it would make it easier for Web hosting services to say, ''Well, it was—Dr. Oz doesn't have any products he sells, so then—how can they run an advertisement saying he's selling this?''

Second idea, we have been—in whistleblower systems that are, in fact, in workplace safety, we have them for financial services. I think honest employees deserve compensation and reward if they help expose illegal behavior by their employers, and I think we ought to incentivize whistleblowers in this space, as well. It's that big of a problem. When I busted those scam artists in San Diego, there were people who worked in that company who knew what they were doing was wrong and might have come forward.

And third, I would argue that we can create a private-sector-funded bounty that would—might help with getting bounty hunters, effectively, on the Web to engage. People who have time and desire and knowledge to go after some of these folks. A lot of times, you know, the people who are victims of these infringements, myself included, many of the people on this panel, would love to do anything we can to empower private citizens to shut down scammers. If it helps the FTC, I think it might be worthwhile, considering a bounty system—again, funded by the private sector—not looking for new laws, nor are we looking for government funding of any of these initiatives.

Senator HELLER. Thank you.

Mr. Haralson, what is your organization, TrustInAds.org, doing to stop these third-parties from placing ads on websites and perhaps those ads that are less truthful?

Mr. HARALSON. Well, again, as I pointed out in my testimony, you know, our companies are deeply incentivized to making sure that these ads stay off of our platforms. I think having user trust in the advertisements that they see is imperative to making sure that the Internet economy and this vibrant advertising ecosystem survives.

When we do—I mean, our companies have very sophisticated automated filtering systems that look for this kind of stuff. And when we do find these types of ads, they're automatically removed, even from our systems, in most cases long before they're actually served by—or seen by users. But, at the same time, as we are notified or we do see bad ads that are on our platforms, they are immediately removed, the advertiser account is reviewed, and appropriate action is taken, when warranted.

Senator HELLER. Thank you.

Mr. Chairman, thank you.

Senator MCCASKILL. Senator Klobuchar.

STATEMENT OF HON. AMY KLOBUCHAR, U.S. SENATOR FROM MINNESOTA

Senator KLOBUCHAR. Thank you very much, Chairman. Thank you for holding this hearing.

Thank you, to all of you.

Yesterday, I looked up the top-selling weight-loss products on Amazon. And even with the FTC's actions against green coffee marketers, green coffee is still a product in the top–20 selling products. The rest of the products are currently Garcinia Cambogia-related products, which I understand was featured on your show, Dr. Oz, but it also was highlighted as a product and that advertisers used to scam consumers by creating a fake website, claiming to be Women's Health magazine.

When it was on your show, did you talk about the side effects? And I know Senator McCaskill has questioned you at length about this. You said this was all 2 years ago, and you're not making these claims anymore. But, what—did you talk about the side effects then? And did the deceptive practices then coming out of that change how you've conducted your shows?

Dr. OZ. So, I actually brought transcripts of these different shows. And we would, in each case, have an expert who spends their entire life dealing with dietary supplements talk about the different products. They review pluses and minuses in most of the—and I just went through and leafed through a few of these pages. But, as—you know, I look at these scripts, and I think to myself, "I wish that they would have just played another 30 seconds of the little clip they used for the advertisements, that they—we often see on the Web."

So, as an example, with the Garcinia show, "I'm going to say something for everyone to hear. Please listen carefully. I don't sell the stuff. I'm not making money on it. I'm not going to mention any brands to you, either, because I don't want you to control.'' I bring that up, because—and, by the way, elsewhere in the segment, I also talked specifically about the fact that, ''If you don't exercise and diet at the same time, it's not going to work. You know, folks, it's just—it's a pill. Don't go home thinking it's just a pill that's going to help you. But, together with the normal, natural things we tell you to do with the foods you eat or healthy lifestyle,'' et cetera. So, we make those points.

You know what the biggest disservice I've done for my audience? It's not the flowery language that Senator McCaskill is criticizing me for. It's that I never told them where to go to buy the products. I wanted to stay above the fray, and I felt, in my own mind, that if I talked about specific companies selling high-quality products, it would seem like I was supporting those companies. And so, I never gave them the—the audience, an idea of where to go to buy the stuff. So, that opened up a huge market for folks to just make—take stuff, real stuff—doesn't, practically, matter—and start to use my name to try to sell. I left my audience hanging, thinking I was doing the ethical thing.

And I firmly believe, if I had gone on and called it a miracle—and again, I'm not—it's not a miracle like it's, you know, going to work every day for the rest of your life for every person, but it's miraculous that something like this is out there, we don't know about it. If I had told them, ''Go buy these four companies' products, because they're the ones that are reputable,'' it would have killed this off. And I blame myself.

Senator KLOBUCHAR. So, what stopped you from doing that, then?

Dr. OZ. I thought that it was commercial, that if I—a doctor shouldn't sell products. You wouldn't trust me if you came to me for advice and I said, ''You know, Senator, you've got, you know, a stubbed toe, here. Take my version of a salving cream, here''—it just doesn't sound and feel right to me. I really feel that—I—in the Internet Age, taking a bricks-and-mortar approach to it doesn't work. And I should have been savvy enough to say to myself—and I kick myself, still—maybe I'll do it in the future—that I should just say, ''Here are the companies I trust. Just go buy their products, because they're not going to scam you, they're not going to make illegal claims.'' If I say that it helps you lose a pound a week for 8 weeks, which is what a trial says, and then someone on the Web takes that and changes it to, you know, 40 pounds in 3 weeks, which you can only really do through an amputation, then all of a sudden, you know, it's like I said those things, and it hurts me and—part of the reason I came today, this is a huge problem for me.

Senator KLOBUCHAR. OK. And I—as someone that's seen these ads, they're very, very seductive, when you're looking through things and trying to figure out what—a good diet plan to go on. And I—I mean, you're going to have two choices, here. Either you don't talk about these things at all that are going to be susceptible to this kind of scam or you're going to have to be more specific, because right now it isn't working. And obviously you're not the only celebrity that has had this happen to them.

And, I guess, Ms. Engle, I'd go back to you on this, is whether or not you think you have enough resources to go after this, what you think of Dr. Fabricant's idea that you shouldn't just be focused on fly-by-nights or—what do we need to do, here, to get a handle on this?

Ms. ENGLE. The FTC does put a lot of resources behind our weight-loss fraud enforcement efforts, and we do pursue both fly-by-night companies and more established companies. The NPB Green—Pure Green Coffee case I mentioned was pretty much a fly-by-night company. We also pursued 11 different companies that were selling acai berry weight-loss products through fake news sites and affiliate marketing over the Internet, in addition to Sensa and some of the other more established companies.

So, you know, we do look across the board. Unfortunately, there are a lot of players in this space. These cases can be time-intensive to investigate. We do look at the studies that are out there, very carefully. We hire experts. Often, the defendants will hire experts. We pay a lot of close attention, because we don't want to—you know, we want to be sure where the science is. We don't want to challenge something as false or misleading if, in fact, it has real efficacy, if the claims are substantiated.

So, the cases are time-intensive, but, you know, we're trying to bring as many of them as possible and to get as much money back for consumers as we can.

Senator KLOBUCHAR. Do you think there should be more FDA regulation of these supplements and these kinds of things? Would that be helpful, beyond the advertising? I know we've had some votes on this and discussed this in Congress.

Ms. ENGLE. Well, I can't—certainly can't speak for the FDA. I understand that they have their hands full with—in the case of dietary supplements, with adulterated products. They've taken number—a number of actions against weight-loss products that actually contain prescription drugs in them, and they're putting their resources there.

Senator KLOBUCHAR. But, do you think that we need a bigger approach to this than just looking at a celebrity list or advertisements if people are falsely relying on claims that aren't true?

Ms. ENGLE. Well, I do think it would be helpful for the—first of all, I think the approach taken by the *TrustInAds.org* organization with Google and the others is quite helpful. I think if—the media could do a better job of screening out these facially false claims, and we're hopeful that the BBB will work with us to better disseminate that and get that message across. And that can help just, you know, eliminate these—some of these ads, at least, from running.

Senator KLOBUCHAR. Thank you.

Senator MCCASKILL. Ms. Engle, I know you've taken a lot of action against various companies—and some of them, fly-by-night—but, what about the media outlets that run these ads? You all have never gone there. Talk about that. Is that an approach that you've considered? Is that one that you have authority to do? If you've got a media outlet that is, you know, particularly using a lot of fraudulent advertising, that appears to be fraudulent on its face, but yet they're not screening them out, why no enforcement action there?

Ms. ENGLE. Well, the media enjoy significant First Amendment protections, so there are certainly those issues if we were to attempt to sue a media company for running a deceptive ad. Section 12 of the FTC Act does actually give us authority to pursue any entity that disseminates a false or misleading ad for a food, drug, device, or a cosmetic. But, we have—really thought it would—make more sense to work with the media voluntarily, cooperatively to— by issuing—actually, this *Gut Check Guide* that we issued earlier this year was a reissuance of the guidance we first issued back in 2003. We called it "Red Flags." And we've renamed it. We had good success at that time, particularly with the magazines, in getting them to stop running ads containing these seven facially—false claims. And we think it—you know, it makes more sense for us to try to work voluntarily with the media.

Senator McCASKILL. Mr. Peeler, I know you've said that some media have done a sophisticated job in screening, and some haven't. Who's doing a good job, here, and who's doing a bad job?

Mr. PEELER. It largely varies by the size of the media. The national broadcast media have historically had very rigorous ad screening programs, so you would not see the types of ads that you were showing today on the national advertising part of the media.

Senator McCASKILL. But, the national—the interesting thing is, those national broadcasting companies own a lot of the cable stations that these ads are appearing on.

Mr. PEELER. And the——

Senator McCASKILL. It's the same ownership.

Mr. PEELER. And the screening that is done for the affiliates and for the cable channels varies. And then, when you get down to smaller media—and I think radio is a good example. It's a local media, the advertising staffs are pretty small, and I think that's where something like what the FTC has just done highlighting seven false weight-loss claims, that even an ad buyer in a very small media could just sit and look at those seven claims and say "yes" for this and "no" for that. A claim that you're never have to diet again or that you can eat all you want and take this pill and lose weight, those claims we still see, and they shouldn't be getting on the media at all.

Senator McCASKILL. But, satellite radio is not local, and they're all over satellite radio.

Mr. PEELER. Yes. There have been a number of changes in the technology that the industry needs to catch up with, you're exactly right.

Senator McCASKILL. So, you didn't want to say satellite radio, you just waited for me to say it.

[Laughter.]

Senator McCASKILL. I do think that there is a problem there.

Mr. PEELER. And I would add that there are really two things to look at in media screening. One is the traditional type of media screening that the broadcast networks do. The second is the program that Rob—Mr. Haralson—just talked about, which is trying to translate that to the new media and look at these claims really not on a text basis, but almost an algorithmic basis. And that's an area that has a lot of promise for real progress.

Senator MCCASKILL. Talk a little bit about the fly-by-nights. I think Dr. Fabricant's point that it's easier to go after L'Occitane and Sensa and companies that you can find that have buildings and that are actually manufacturing something and putting their label on it, than these post office boxes. And that's one of our conundrums in consumer protection in this subcommittee. So many hearings we've had, whether it's robocalls or other topics we've had hearings on, finding the post office box or finding the IP address, and taking action against those who are responsible, is very complicated in this world, especially when it—you're looking at technology, in terms of IP addresses that certainly many of them are not sited in this country. Tell me about what kind of resources you may need, or that you don't have, to do a better job after the fly-by-nights.

Ms. ENGLE. Yes. So, you're absolutely right. I mean, when you see an ad on the Internet—so, for us, the first thing is to try to figure out who's behind that ad. And it's not actually easy to do. What we're seeing a lot nowadays is that—you know, that some company will be working with a number of affiliate marketers through an affiliate network, and so there is a whole host of different companies that are actually placing the little ads that you see. And then, when the consumer clicks on it, you know, one tiny trip—tip to a flat belly, or something like that—one weird old trick, you know, to lose weight, something like that—the consumer clicks on that, and, if they buy the product, then that affiliate gets paid, but that's not actually the company that's selling the product. There's another company who's behind the product. And it requires us to send out multiple rounds of subpoenas to the Web hosters and to the ad networks to try to figure out who's behind this, and then—and that was what we did, actually, in the acai berry sweep. And it—you know, it takes a significant amount of resources. We're able to do it. We have compulsory process authority—that is, we can subpoena this information. But, it is time-consuming.

Senator MCCASKILL. Well, what about the middleman, here? Have you gone after the middleman, the ones that are actually— the affiliates that you talk about that are actually the ones that are moving these ads around the Internet, and then they are really a conduit to the actual product company that is behind the curtain? Have you taken action against those folks that are actually placing the "one secret to get rid of your belly fat"?

Ms. ENGLE. Yes, we have. We have gone after affiliates. And one of the issues there is—and we've gone after some large affiliates— but, one of the issues there is, when we go in, we never know who—how big the company is. And sometimes it turns out they're quite small, or they haven't made many sales, and it's not worth pursuing. But, we have gone after the larger affiliates, as well. We've gone after every player in the ecosystem.

Mr. PEELER. And, Senator McCaskill, could I add that, for all frauds, the BBB system, with 100 offices around the country, gets about a million complaints and provides a service for consumers, where you can go and check and see what types of complaints a company is getting. And, as I said in my testimony, very often misleading performance of claims are also accompanied by bad refund policies and negative-option shipping policies. The St. Louis Better

Business Bureau had one of these companies that was just billing people sort of randomly for the products. So, if the consumers will go to the BBB website before they buy and check and see what type of complaint history this company has, it will help. It won't eliminate the problem, but it would help, and help protect them.

Senator McCASKILL. Senator Heller?

Senator HELLER. Thank you.

Ms. Engle, I want to know a little bit more about your recent consent orders it announced as part of the Operation Failed Resolution. The FTC is now barring defendants from making certain claims unless they have at least two adequate and well-controlled human clinical studies. Is that accurate?

Ms. ENGLE. Yes. Those cases all required the companies under order to have at least two well-controlled studies to support weight-loss claims, going forward.

Senator HELLER. It's my understanding that the FTC has also tried to apply that elsewhere. And even though there are some current guidelines in the agency that states that determining whether competent and reliable scientific evidence exists is a flexible and a fact-specific inquiry, do you have conflicts? Or are you applying this new standard elsewhere? And is there a conflict in some of the regulations that you're trying to enforce?

Ms. ENGLE. I don't see any conflict. The—so, the basic law is that companies must have a reasonable basis for the advertising claims that they make at the time they make those claims. What constitutes a reasonable basis will depend on the product and the claim. In the case of products that promise health benefits, the Commission has required competent and reliable scientific evidence. And then, again, what constitutes competent and reliable scientific evidence will vary depending upon the claim. So, for example, a claim that a product will prevent cancer or treat cancer, for example, will require a higher level of evidence than a claim that a product, you know, will smooth dry skin.

So, in the case of weight-loss products, in particular, based on the factors we consider, in consultation with experts, we've determined that randomized controlled clinical studies are needed in order to substantiate a claim that a given product will cause weight loss.

The Commission has required two of these studies in its orders. Now, it's not—I'm not saying that if a company came to us and had one good study on weight loss, we would say, "Oh, that claim is not substantiated." But, once we have determined that a company has violated the FTC Act, has made unsubstantiated weight-loss claims and they are now under order, we have put in a requirement that, going forward, they should have two studies. And these kinds of studies for weight loss do not need to be particularly long term, they're not particularly expensive, relative to the amount of money that can be made for these products. And, given the level of fraud that we have seen in this area, it's important to have the extra assurance of a second study to assure that, you know, this is a real result, that this wasn't due to some fluke or inadvertent bias or something like that in the study.

Senator HELLER. Let's talk about your dietary supplement guidelines. We have not revised that or repudiated some of those guidelines, even though there are some parts of those guidelines that seem or appear to be inconsistent with the FTC's current stance, as we just mentioned, about competent, reliable scientific evidence. Do you see it that way?

Ms. ENGLE. No, I don't see a conflict, because the dietary supplement guidelines are written broadly to cover the full range of dietary supplements that may be offered and the full range of claims that may be made for them. So, the guidance is written more broadly. And then, again, when we're in the context of a specific case in a specific investigation of a product, we know what claims were made for them, what the ingredients are, and then we have a record on which to base order requirements for substantiations for claims, going forward.

Senator HELLER. Is there any intention of modifying those guidelines?

Ms. ENGLE. Well, there has been some discussion of just looking at them—they—oh, gosh, they're, I think, 13 years old now, maybe—to see, you know, what—if they need to be freshened up. But, again, I don't think there's a conflict between what they say at all and what we're doing in our orders.

Senator HELLER. OK. Thank you.

Thank you.

Senator MCCASKILL. Senator Klobuchar.

Senator KLOBUCHAR. Thank you.

And, Mr. Haralson, I want to talk to you a little bit about the work that you're doing.

Mr. HARALSON. Sure.

Senator KLOBUCHAR. And I was just looking at my Twitter account and found about four of these ads about these things, like how many cups of coffee I can drink in one day to lose 2 pounds—that was pretty good—and various other things on fat melting and other things. And I understand that your member companies permanently suspend advertiser accounts if the severity of the violation of the ad policy is high. What does that mean? How many ad accounts have been permanently suspended? Are there temporary suspensions? And how do you handle this?

Mr. HARALSON. Well, again, I think every company that's within *TrustInAds.org* has different approaches and different policies in place to address these. However, again, it depends on the severity of the violation or if there are multiple violations. But, there are options where companies—the member companies may, for example, work with the advertiser to fix the ad to make sure that it is in compliance with their ads policies. There is an option to remove those ads. And then, the third option, obviously, for—certainly, for egregious violations, is to suspend the advertiser account.

But, interestingly enough, some of the sophisticated scammers will immediately try to open new accounts and try to push their ads again through these filtering systems. So, it becomes a little bit of a cat-and-mouse game.

Senator KLOBUCHAR. And when you say it's easier to target vulnerable populations through online advertising than some of the more traditional methods or—and do you think more online companies are going to be—I think sometimes, with online, they think it's a personal message to them. These are often just from people——

Mr. HARALSON. Well, I think that these types of scams attract the largest constituencies as possible, be it weight loss, hair loss, whatever you name it. And again, I think that we're seeing these types of ads across the board, both in print—or in print media and online.

Senator KLOBUCHAR. OK. How about the protection of data? I mean, more and more, we're using data collection, things like Fitbit—I have my—I hope that's not deceptive. I think it's pretty good.

[Laughter.]

Senator KLOBUCHAR. And, of course, people are getting all their data collected now on—through this. And it's been actually—I think it's a pretty interesting way to use, sort of, self-motivation to get yourself to exercise and other things. And are companies protecting consumer data to make sure it doesn't fall into the hands of scammers? What's going on in that front?

Mr. HARALSON. Well, I—for example, I'm not familiar with if Fitbit collects the data that is on the device that's on your wrist. I'm—but, as—and I'm a little—can you repeat the question, or just clarify the question a little bit?

Senator KLOBUCHAR. The question is about—more and more, the diet data is going online. People are entering things in, just like they're entering other things in. And has there been an effort by your member companies to look at how you're going to protect that data? And maybe someone else can better answer that.

Mr. HARALSON. Well, I'd—again, I'm not—to my knowledge, I don't believe that our member companies are collecting third-party data particular to health-related devices or whatever the case may be. So—but, I'm happy to——

Senator KLOBUCHAR. And we—it's a whole 'nother issue of some of the popup ads that you get when you start using products. So—and in a way, that some of them are collecting it, because then you can get popup ads about things related to it. But—yes.

Mr. PEELER. And, Senator Klobuchar, there is a fairly broad coalition, called the Digital Advertising Alliance, that is looking at the question of collection of data across sites and doing some pretty significant binary work. The organization was formed, really, at the request of the Federal Trade Commission, to look at exactly those issues.

The specific issue that you're talking about, which is special restrictions on sensitive data about health, is one of the things that's still under development. That's a fairly tricky issue to get everybody in the industry onboard with. But, there is an organization that's been formed, working very effectively in looking at all those issues.

Senator KLOBUCHAR. So, I'm thinking about all the new money that's being spent on all these products as people are, you know, desperately looking at ways to lose weight. And yet, since the 1960s, adult obesity has more than doubled, leading to healthcare challenges for our country, as we know. We know some of these diets are legitimate and well-researched, and some of them aren't. But, what really bothers me, at its core, is that, while for the first time we saw leveling out for kids—not really a big reduction, but a leveling out of the increase in obesity this last year —we're hop-

78

ing some having to do with the work of the First Lady and the work of some of the school lunch programs, which I don't think we should be rolling back those standards, but that's a whole nother— another topic.

What do you think we should be doing to really get people being able to spend their money on what works and what doesn't? We have to admit, here, that we have a major problem when people are spending more and more money and they're gaining more and more weight.

Mr. PEELER. And, you know, that is precisely the type of thing that advertisers that sell and market products that do work worry about. One advertiser comes to mind. He sells fitness equipment, and people say, "We watch the ads, you start sweating while you're watching the ads," because it's very clear that you have to have a dedicated regime, and stick with it. This advertiser loses sales to these——

Senator KLOBUCHAR. Right.

Mr. PEELER.—fraudulent products, because people say, "Well, why would I exercise"——

Senator KLOBUCHAR. Right.

Mr. PEELER.—"for 45 minutes if I can just take a pill and never diet again?"

Senator KLOBUCHAR. Right, exactly. So, your answer would be to be more intense about going after these fraudulent products. And I—that's why I keep going back to, not just the advertising, but the FDA and trying to just get some of them off the market.

Mr. PEELER. Yes. And I think that there's a big role that the types of self-regulatory programs—that two-thirds of the table is talking about—can play to supplement the resources that the government has. What we see is a lot of cases, where, when we contact the advertiser—and we do it fairly quickly—they just say, "Oh, we'll change that claim." We have a fairly high record of success, and that's that many fewer cases that the FDA or the FTC have to deal with.

Mr. HARALSON. Senator, if it would be possible for me to add— I mean, one thing, I think, that makes it difficult is the fact that a lot of these—it's not illegal to sell these products. I think when it becomes illegal is when you're doing it under false claims. And so, for our companies that clearly—some of these claims that are fraudulent violate our ads policies. But, again, it makes it difficult to substantiate the good advertisers versus the bad advertisers because of the sophistication of some of these scammers in the language that they're using and in the ways that they're to circumvent our systems to be able to——

Senator KLOBUCHAR. Right.

Mr. HARALSON.—get their ads served online.

Senator KLOBUCHAR. Understand. Very good.

Well, I think, to me, it means we need some more standards and resources. And we appreciate your efforts trying to monitor them.

Thank you.

Senator McCASKILL. Senator Blumenthal.

STATEMENT OF HON. RICHARD BLUMENTHAL,
U.S. SENATOR FROM CONNECTICUT

Senator BLUMENTHAL. Thank you, Madam Chairman.

Dr. Oz, I want to pursue a question that Senator Klobuchar raised. I understand that it's not your policy to support any particular brands, and that you feel now, as you said to her in response to one of her questions, that perhaps is a mistake. So, I'm wondering, would you consider creating a sort of master list of brands that would be helpful to consumers? Because, after all, you have the immense power of your voice and credibility that would be helpful to consumers if you created such a master list of brands that you feel do work and are helpful.

Dr. Oz. I would love to do that. And I've been speaking to people who I trust in the industry about how to go about it. My best estimates—and I'd love for other industry members to offer this—is that probably 80 percent of the products which are made by 20 percent of the companies are high-quality, reputable products by people who really do their homework and are audited in many different ways, good manufacturing processes and the like. And then 20 percent of the products are made by, you know, a lot of the companies—theoretically, 80 percent—who really aren't that good. They're fly-by-nights. The quality issues are a major concern. The post office box example Dr. Peeler —Mr. Peeler gave is a good example. When I busted these folks in San Diego. I went to their listed address. It's a post office box. So, you really could never find anybody.

So, I—I've been actively looking at that. With your suggestion of support, I think I'm going to do it. And I think it'll do a lot to drain the swamp that we've created around this area.

Senator BLUMENTHAL. Well, I would encourage you to do it. Draining a swamp is really very, very important, because, in this area, as you know, and I think many of us know—I was attorney general of a State for 20 years. I did a lot of work in this area. And if there is any area where consumers are most susceptible and vulnerable to misleading and false pitches, I think it is this one, because their hopes are so high and their needs often are so great. So, I think that would be a welcome development.

I introduced a measure called the Dietary Supplement Labeling Act, along with Senator Durbin, last August. And this bill would require dietary supplement manufacturers to register their products with the FDA and disclose the known risks of their ingredients on a product's label. And I think that this kind of measure is crucial to provide information to consumers regarding dietary supplements and help the FDA identify potential health concerns. And, as you've suggested, a master list of celebrity endorsements might be helpful for the FTC to identify violators, and this bill would create a master list of dietary supplements, similar to that one, that could cause adverse effects, to help consumers understand the risks.

What are your thoughts on that legislation?

Dr. Oz. I think it's a very wise place for us to invest resources. Some of these dietary supplements, especially the ones that are stimulatory supplements, raise great concerns for me. They're often adulterated, even though they claim they're, you know, not working that way. It—that has been a proven way of getting weight loss. You put a amphetamine-type product in a drug—in a product, and it'll work with weight loss, but the side effects are just too great for us to tolerate as a population.

Senator BLUMENTHAL. That method of weight loss may actually be unhealthful.

Dr. OZ. Oh, it has been proven to be unhelpful, which is why the FDA has pulled those products off the market. That's also part of the challenge we face. We are in a time in our history where we're getting closer to having FDA-approved drugs that work in this area. We have a few now, but we've had, you know, very, very few for many, many years. And so, as we get better prescription products that would be effective, then more medicine will turn in that direction.

But, even the very basic techniques that we know work —bariatric surgery, which we way underperform in this country, is very effective. But, people don't want to go that far even though, if you're 100 pounds overweight at age 50, you have the same mortality rate as if you have cancer. So, these are desperate situations with desperate people who are looking for solutions, and that's a recipe for problems.

So, I strongly support the need to look at whether the products are safe, or not. And the other side of the equation is trying to find, you know, ways of getting people ideas that they can use to jumpstart their way back.

Senator BLUMENTHAL. Ms. Engle, let me ask you. Would the FTC find that kind of list helpful?

Ms. ENGLE. Well, the Commission itself has not taken a position on that legislation. Speaking for myself, I think it could be helpful. I think it could be helpful to FDA, certainly, in its law enforcement efforts and providing—it would provide consumers with useful information.

Senator BLUMENTHAL. Thank you.

Thank you all for being here, and thank you for your great work. Thank you.

Senator MCCASKILL. I just want to briefly follow up. I don't know if anyone else has another follow-up. I want to make sure—I appreciate, Dr. Oz, that—we've covered a lot of ground this morning, and a significant part of it was about some of your language you've used in association with some of these products on your show. And you indicated that the products I talked about in my previous questioning, you had—that those shows were a couple of years ago. Well, 3 weeks ago, I quote you, ''FBX literally flushes fat from your system.'' ''Every time you cheat on your diet, I want you to grab one of these tiny, itty-bitty pills. This tiny tablet can push a lot of fat out of your belly.''

People want to believe they can take an itty-bitty pill to push fat out of their body. They want to believe that. And it seems to me that, instead, if you said, ''Every time you cheat on your diet, I want you to take a walk,'' that would eliminate the problem that is at the root of this hearing today. That is that your credibility is being maligned by fraudsters, and, frankly, being threatened by a notion that anybody can take an itty-bitty pill to flush fat out of their system.

In January, you called Forskolin, quote, ''lightning in a bottle'' and ''a miracle flower to fight fat.'' That was just in January.

I know you know how much power you have. I know you know that. You are very powerful. And with power comes a great deal of responsibility. And I know you take it seriously, and I know you care about your listening audience and your viewing audience. I know you care about America's health. And you are being made an example of today because of the power you have in this space. And we didn't call this hearing to beat up on you, but we did call this hearing to talk about a real crisis in consumer protection. And you can either be part of the police, here, or you can be part of the problem. And we're just hopeful that you will do a better job at being part of the police.

Dr. Oz. Well, I came here because I want to be part of the solution, not part of the problem.

You mentioned FBX, which is basically a fiber. And we know that fiber, when taken correctly, has been a very effective tool for weight loss, for the reason that I stated.

Your comments about the language I use is well heard, and I appreciate it. I host a daytime television show, where I feel a need to bring passion into people's lives about what they can do. And I'm very respectful of the fact that, when it's used—and it has been used—as a way of defrauding people, that it's a harmful process.

And I appreciate your kind words about the power I have. I'm in a situation where I'm second-guessing every word I use on the show right now. FBX is used by my family. I do think it's important. I do think if you cheat on a meal, it's worth including some fiber. That's why we tell people to eat vegetables when they go out for a big meal, because it serves that very purpose.

So, I'm—you know, I have things that I think work for people. I want them to try them, just to help them feel better so they can keep doing the other things that we spend every single day on the show talking about. And when I feel, as a host of a show, that I can't use words that are flowery that are, you know, exultatory, I feel, you know, like I've been disenfranchised, like my power's been taken away to get people. You don't want to be in a pulpit talking about how passionate you are about life and thinking, ''Well, you know, if I use that word, it's going to be quoted back to me.'' And yes, the 100 words around it are all about doing other things right.

So, I'm very respectful. I've heard the message. I've told my colleagues at the FTC: I get it.

Senator MCCASKILL. OK, good.

I want to see all that passion and that floweriness about the beauty of a walk at sunset or——

[Laughter.]

Dr. Oz. OK.

Senator MCCASKILL.—you know, the——

Dr. Oz. Touché.

Senator MCCASKILL.—how you feel when you get off the bike in the morning——

Dr. Oz. OK.

Senator MCCASKILL.—and, I mean, no one's telling you not to use passion. But, passion in connection with the word ''miracle pill'' and ''weight loss'' is a recipe for disaster in this environment, in

82

terms of the people who are looking for an easy fix and getting sometimes, I think, delusional about whether or not an easy fix is going to be there for them. So——

And I appreciate everyone being here. Does anybody else have anything else?

Senator KLOBUCHAR. Well, I was going to say that we all experience the feeling, as elected officials, of any word that can be taken out of context.

[Laughter.]

Senator KLOBUCHAR. We kind of can relate to this.

[Laughter.]

Senator MCCASKILL. We feel——

Senator KLOBUCHAR. But, at the same time, in addition to being a celebrity, you're a doctor, and I just believe that doctors have this duty, as we believe we have to represent the people we represent—you have the duty to give them the best evidence. And when stuff is being taken out of context, like it has, or, you have admitted making mistakes in how you described a few things, I think you have a duty to correct that record, and then be careful, going forward, because you can use your knowledge and your celebrity status to do good things. And right now, to me, it seems like we're going to the opposite way, here. So——

Dr. OZ. Well, Senator, just—again, I don't want to rehash this, but, as a good example, I did a whole show around how green coffee bean extract and the way it was described was not the right way to do it. I, you know, in fact, brought audience members in, did a several-month program to sort of see if it worked or not. It has no impact. I—the things I have said continue to be used——

Senator KLOBUCHAR. Right.

Dr. OZ.—as weapons against the public.

Senator KLOBUCHAR. Understand. But, I think that continual debunking of some of this is helpful, and the emphasis on what works best. And you know it better than us, so we appreciate it if you'd keep focusing on that.

Senator MCCASKILL. Thank you all.

Senator BLUMENTHAL. I think, Dr. Oz, if you ever need anyone to fill on your——

[Laughter.]

Dr. OZ. I know who to call.

Senator BLUMENTHAL. I'm sure you'd have a few takers in this body.

[Laughter.]

Dr. OZ. Thank you, Senator Blumenthal.

Senator MCCASKILL. Thank you all very much.

[Whereupon, at 11:15 a.m., the hearing was adjourned.]

APPENDIX

WRITTEN TESTIMONY OF THE ELECTRONIC RETAILING ASSOCIATION

Submitted by: Julie Coons, President and CEO and Bill McClellan, Vice President, Government Affairs,
Electronic Retailing Association

Introduction

Chairman McCaskill, Ranking Member Heller and Members of the Committee, the Electronic Retailing Association ("ERA") thanks you for the opportunity to submit this written testimony on how to protect consumers from false and deceptive advertising of weight-loss products. We strongly applaud your oversight and interest in this important topic to ensure that our Nation's consumers are protected from bad actors.

The Electronic Retailing Association (ERA) is the trade association in the United States and abroad that represents leaders of the direct-to-consumer marketplace, which includes members that utilize electronic retailing on television, radio and online to engage with consumers. Today, ERA proudly represents more than 400 companies in countries around the world including many of the industry's most prominent retail merchants. ERA's membership consists of a diverse ecosystem of businesses and entrepreneurs operating at the cutting edge of innovation who have adapted to the rapidly evolving challenges found in the current retail landscape.

In 2004 the ERA board of directors partnered with the Council of Better Business Bureaus, Inc. (CBBB) and the Advertising Self-Regulatory Council (ASRC) to create the Electronic Retailing Self-Regulation Program (ERSP). ERSP was created specifically to improve consumer confidence and demonstrate to the Federal Trade Commission (FTC) and Congress that ERA is committed to helping companies within the industry comply with existing regulations. The program strives to provide a quick and efficient process to review egregious advertising claims and to alert members, and in some cases the FTC, of noncompliant companies. We believe that ERSP creates a level playing field for direct-to-consumer commerce industry professionals and through the years has increased industry credibility and pride.

The FTC has reviewed our efforts and is generally very favorable of ERSP, as they share our frustration that a few bad players taint the direct response industry. However, the FTC has made it clear, that ERA members should not consider ERSP a "free pass." In other words, advertising that meets the standards of the ERSP review process may still be subject to challenge by the FTC and others.

To date ERSP results have been impressive in removing deceptive and misleading advertising campaigns from the air as the following program statistics indicate.

ERSP Statistics
Updated May 2, 2014

Total Direct Response Advertising Tracked	12,600
Home Shopping Reports	30
Total Cases Current and Closed	349
Average Case Length (Calendar Days)	71 days
Cases from Monitoring	187
Cases from Consumer Challenges *	34
Cases from Competitor Challenges *	102
Compliance Cases	26
Advertising Modified or Discontinued	318
FTC Nonparticipation Referrals	27
Compliance Referral to FTC	3

While the ERSP program has received praise from all quarters, we know there is more work to be done. On April 26, 2006 then FTC Chairwoman Deborah Platt Majoras delivered a speech to industry participants entitled "Self-Regulation in the Infomercial Industry: Moving Forward". We believe that Commissioner Majoras' remarks remain relevant today. The vast majority of marketers have stepped up to the plate and delivered meaningful and voluntary self-regulation. The small fraction of marketers who refuse to participate in ERSP proceedings or comply with ERSP decisions are referred to the FTC for enforcement action. We continue our efforts to urge more cable companies and other media outlets to support these efforts by closely monitoring ERSP decisions and utilizing past case history to make current clearance decisions. Some have chosen to do so while others have not. We look forward to working with the Committee on strategies to remove deceptive and misleading weight-loss claims from the marketplace as embodied in the FTC's "Gut Check" guidance. However, it is important to ensure that any action taken does not have an unintended chilling effect that punishes those who are doing the right thing. Companies who are offering legitimate products that are designed to combat the growing national obesity epidemic marketed with lawful messages should not be penalized for fear that their advertising copy will not be cleared. ERA and its members stand ready to assist both the FTC and the Committee as we continue our collective work to ensure a healthy and vibrant marketplace for all.

RESPONSE TO WRITTEN QUESTIONS SUBMITTED BY HON. DEAN HELLER TO
MARY KOELBEL ENGLE

Question 1. In your testimony before the Committee, you state that "in the case of weight loss claims, in particular, based on the factors we consider and in consultation with experts, we have determined that randomized controlled clinical studies are needed in order to substantiate a claim that a given product will cause weight loss." This statement appears to be inconsistent with existing Commission guidance that states, with respect to health claims, "[t]here is no fixed formula for the number or type of studies required." What is the Federal Trade Commission's position on what constitutes "competent and reliable scientific evidence" needed to substantiate weight loss claims?

Answer. The Commission's dietary supplement guidance referred to in the question is a guidance document laying out overarching advertising interpretation and substantiation principles with respect to health-related claims generally. The guidance provided is necessarily more general than the analysis the Commission conducts when it has before it particular claims for particular products. In law enforcement investigations, the Commission uses six factors (the "*Pfizer* factors") to determine what constitutes appropriate substantiation for particular advertising claims in the case before it. These factors include: (1) the type of product advertised; (2) the type of claim; (3) the benefits of a truthful claim; (4) the cost of developing substantiation for the claim; (5) the consequences of a false claim; and (6) the amount of substantiation that experts in the field would require.[1] Using this standard, rigorous evidence is required to substantiate weight-loss claims. First, the Commission requires a high level of substantiation—competent and reliable scientific evidence—for products involving health or safety, and products promoted for weight loss clearly involve health benefits. Second, for various reasons, including the placebo effect, it is difficult for consumers to evaluate the truth or falsity of weight loss claims. In addition, weight-loss claims often refer to facts and figures (*e.g* lose X pounds in Y weeks), also the kind of claim for which the Commission requires tests or studies sufficient to support the specific figures. With regard to the third and fourth elements, which are usually considered together, the benefits of a truthful claim would be substantial, and the market for an effective product would be enormous. Moreover, the cost of conducting studies is reasonable when compared to the potential economic benefit and therefore should not deter the development of new products. For example, a twelve-week clinical weight-loss study can be conducted for approximately $300,000, while a weight-loss product advertising campaign can generate tens or even hundreds of millions of dollars in revenue. Fifth, the economic harm from fraudulent weight loss products is substantial. For example, the sales of Sensa from 2008 through 2012 totaled over $364 million. Sixth, the kind of study experts would require may vary with the type of weight-loss product or service at issue. For example, a different type of study may be appropriate for a weight-loss clinic that has access to patient files than to a dietary supplement or an exercise device. For dietary supplements, experts would generally require randomized, well-controlled clinical studies.[2]

---

[1] *See Pfizer*, 81 F.T.C. 23, 64 (1972); *Thompson Medical Co.*, 104 F.T.C. 648, 821 (1984).
[2] *See FTC* v. *Nat'l Urological Group*, 645 F. Supp. 2d 1167, 1202 (N.D. Ga. 2008); *FTC* v. *Slim America*, 77 F. Supp. 2d 1263, 1273 (S.D. Fla. 1999); *Schering Corp.*, 118 F.T.C. 1030, 1116 (1994) (ALJ, Initial Decision).

Question 2. In your testimony, you state that the adequate and well-controlled human studies the FTC requires to substantiate weight-loss claims are ''not particularly expensive relative to the amount of money that can be made for these products.'' Please provide the basis for this assertion.

Answer. Experts the FTC staff has consulted have indicated that a well-controlled clinical trial of reasonable size and duration (for example, 100 subjects over twelve weeks) can be conducted for approximately $300,000. Even if the cost were higher, it would still be only a small fraction of the amount that weight loss marketers spend on their advertising campaigns and an even smaller fraction of the revenue generated by a successful weight-loss advertising campaign.

Question 3. Some observers have stated that the FTC's requirement of two well-controlled human studies will create a very high barrier to entry that will preclude small businesses from entering the marketplace and stifle innovation on products Americans want. Has the Commission's Bureau of Economics been consulted for its view on potential competitive effects of such a requirement?

Answer. As noted in the answer to question 1 above, the FTC does not have an across-the-board requirement of two well-controlled human studies to substantiate health-related claims. Rather, the level of substantiation depends on an analysis of the *Pfizer* factors.[3] As for weight-loss order requiring two controlled trials, please see the answer to question 5 below.

The concern that imposing a rigorous standard of substantiation will result in fewer entrants to the marketplace or stifle innovation is unwarranted for several reasons. First, strong order provisions requiring solid scientific evidence safeguards consumers from companies that have engaged in deceptive advertising in the past by ensuring that future claims by these specific companies are truthful.

Second, the problem with the current marketplace, particularly for weight loss products, is not that there are too few entrants, but that too many companies are flooding the marketplace with exaggerated claims based on preliminary or weak evidence or even hearsay about the latest fad ingredient. This view is shared by many in the industry and was expressed by industry representatives at the hearing.[4] Responsible supplement marketers and their trade associations have repeatedly sought tougher enforcement by both FDA and the FTC to crack down on unfounded claims and have even funded programs with the Council of Better Business Bureaus to increase self-regulation.[5] As CRN's President stated at the hearing, ''Responsible firms, like CRN's members, suffer along with consumers as legal, reasonable, and defensible advertising for weight management claims gets dwarfed by outlandish claims that violate the law and deceive consumers.''[6]

The harm is not just economic, as discussed in the response to question 1 above, but also health-related. Unsubstantiated promises of dramatic and easy weight loss lure consumers away from proven, but more difficult, methods for managing weight. Given the option of taking a pill or cutting calories and exercising daily, many consumers will opt for the pill. With the number of deaths related to poor diet and inactivity increasing and estimated to overtake tobacco soon as the leading cause of death,[7] the harm caused by false claims for ineffective diet pills is real and substantial.

The Commission's Bureau of Economics participates in investigations and has an opportunity to provide a formal opinion to the Commission that includes its assessment of the merits of the case and the appropriateness of the remedies. A central part of our economists' analysis is the impact of the order on the marketplace. If the Bureau of Economics believes that there is a potential of competitive harm from requiring two-well controlled human clinical studies in a particular case, it will advise the Commission of its view.

Question 4. The FTC's current guidance, *Dietary Supplements: An Advertising Guide for Industry,* states that animal and *in vitro* studies are appropriate ''particu-

---

[3] In the context of a remedial order, the Commission may also fashion fencing-in relief considering such factors as the deliberateness of the violation, the violator's past history with respect to advertising practices, and the transferability of the challenged practices to other claims or products. *Removatron Int'l Corp.* v. *FTC,* 884 F.2d 1489, 1498–99 (1st Cir. 1989); *Sterling Drug* v. *FTC,* 741 F.2d 1146, 1155 (9th Cir. 1984).

[4] *See, e.g.,* Written Testimony of Steve Mister, President and CEO of the Council for Responsible Nutrition (June 17, 2014) at 4–5 (supporting the FTC's numerous enforcement actions against deceptive weight loss advertising, while comparing enforcement to the carnival game ''whack-a-mole,'' with two more examples of deceptive advertising popping up for every case the FTC targets).

[5] *Id.* at 5–6.

[6] *Id.* at 5.

[7] See Report on the Dietary Guidelines Advisory Committee on the Dietary Guidelines for Americans, 2010 (June 15, 2010), B1–1, available at *http://www.DietaryGuidelines.gov.*

larly where they are widely considered to be acceptable substitutes for human research or where human research is infeasible.'' Yet in its recent consent decrees, the Commission has imposed language requiring human clinical studies.

Answer. The Dietary Supplement Advertising Guide makes clear in the same paragraph that, ''[a]s a general rule, well-controlled human clinical studies are the most reliable form of evidence.'' The Commission's recent orders requiring human clinical studies are each based on a careful analysis of the *Pfizer* factors referenced above, including the type of product, the specific claims being challenged as false or unsubstantiated, and the amount and type of evidence that experts in the relevant field believe is reasonable. In every instance where the Commission's order has required human clinical studies, there has been no basis to conclude that animal or *in vitro* studies are acceptable substitutes for human research.

Question 4a. With respect to health-benefit claims, including weight-loss claims, how does the Commission determine whether human research is infeasible?

Answer. Commission staff makes that determination through an analysis of the *Pfizer* factors and in consultation with experts in the relevant field of research. This consultation includes a review of the existing body of scientific literature related to the challenged claims.

Question 4b. How does the Commission determine whether animal, in vitro, or other studies are acceptable substitutes for human research?

Answer. Again, the Commission staff makes that determination through an analysis of the *Pfizer* factors and in consultation with experts in the relevant field of research.

Question 4c. Are human clinical trials practical for all health-benefit claims, including weight loss claims?

Answer. Human clinical studies are feasible and are the widely-accepted level of evidence necessary for demonstrating the efficacy of weight loss products. Likewise, for most other health benefit claims challenged in Commission cases, human research is feasible and the accepted level of evidence. The guides set out examples of limited situations where human clinical trials may not be feasible. For example, a clinical study may not be possible to establish the relationship between a nutrient and the reduced risk of developing a health condition that takes years to manifest itself. In such a case, where a clinical intervention trial would be difficult and prohibitively costly, the Commission has indicated that it will consider epidemiologic evidence as an acceptable substitute for clinical data. Example 14 of the Dietary Supplements Advertising Guide illustrates this situation.

Question 5. Once the FTC Act enters into a consent decree with a company regarding unsubstantiated weight-loss claims, the FTC has required that the company possess at least two adequate and well-controlled human clinical studies to substantiate future weight-loss claims. In other words, the FTC is imposing a requirement of a higher degree of certainty, even though the claims may be otherwise truthful and substantiated.

Answer. The Commission has wide discretion in determining the scope of an order necessary to remedy the illegal practices it has found, and it is well-established that the Commission may impose ''fencing-in relief'' to help ensure future compliance with the law. *See, e.g., FTC* v. *Ruberoid Co.*, 343 U.S. 470, 473 (1952); *FTC* v. *Colgate-Palmolive Co.*, 380 U.S. 374, 392 (1965); *Removatron Int'l Corp.* v. *FTC*, 884 F.2d 1489, 1498–99 (1st Cir. 1989); *Stouffer Foods Corp.* 118 F.T.C. 746, 811 (1994). In determining the scope of fencing-in relief, the Commission considers such factors as the seriousness and deliberateness of the violation; the ease with which the violative claim may be transferred to other products; and whether the advertiser has a history of prior violations. *See, e.g., Removatron*, 884 F.2d at 1498–99 (upholding well-controlled clinical testing requirement as reasonable fencing-in); *Stouffer Foods Corp.* 118 F.T.C. at 811.

Question 5a. Why are results from one study insufficient, even if they are fully controlled and independent?

Answer. Recent Commission orders have required that weight loss claims be supported by at least two adequate and well-controlled clinical studies. This requirement is applicable only to the company under order and only to the specific claims covered by that order provision. It does not necessarily apply to firms not under order. The Commission imposes the two-study requirement based on a case-specific factual determination of the nature of the violation.

The need for a second study conforms to well-recognized scientific principles favoring replication of study results to establish a causal relationship between exposure to a substance and a health outcome.[8] Replication is important to reduce the potential for systematic bias, either intended or unintended. Any clinical trial, even when conducted by parties independent of the product manufacturer, may be subject to unanticipated, undetected, systematic biases that operate despite the best intentions of sponsors and investigators, leading to flawed conclusions. Replication of results also reduces the likelihood that the findings are attributable to chance or random error and provides additional confidence in the validity of the findings.

Question 5b. When the FTC applies this heightened substantiation requirement in a consent order, is it permissible for the Commission to prohibit (or "fence in") conduct beyond the scope of the alleged violation?

Answer. The Commission has the discretion to issue orders containing "fencing-in" provisions that are "broader than the conduct that is declared unlawful." [9] The two-study requirement typically applies to the specific weight loss or health claims challenged in the complaint and other closely-related claims. Broader fencing-in provisions governing substantiation of other health benefits, performance, and efficacy claims typically apply the more general standard of "competent and reliable scientific evidence."

Question 5c. How does the FTC determine the scope of products and claims to which the "two adequate and well-controlled human clinical study" requirement should apply?

Answer. The Commission carefully considers the nature of the particular claims alleged to be deceptive in the Commission's complaint and tailors the order, including the remedy or relief, such as a two-study requirement, to ensure that the order is reasonably related to the conduct giving rise to the violation and that it is consistent with specific facts of the case and the level of evidence that experts in the field would consider reasonable and appropriate for the particular claims and products covered by the order.

Question 6. Your statement to the Committee that multiple studies are needed "given the level of fraud that we have seen in this area," appears to justify the Commission's application of heightened substantiation requirements on grounds that weight-loss-related fraud is particularly high; however, health care claims (which include, *inter alia,* weight-loss scams) rank relatively low among the types of complaints received by the FTC, falling outside the top-ten consumer complaints and comprise about two percent of total complaints received, according to the most-recent *Consumer Sentinel Network Data Book.* Because weight-loss claims are reported as a subset of the complaint category, it would appear weight-loss claims on their own rank even lower. Is it the practice of the Commission to impose heightened requirements in accordance with the level of fraud in a particular area?

Answer. My statement about the "level of fraud that we have seen in this area" as a factor in determining the appropriate level of substantiation was a reference to my written testimony about the instances of outright fraud that the FTC staff has uncovered in the course of our investigations of weight loss marketing by companies now under order.[10] I indicated that the Commission has found troubling practices in more than one weight loss case where the company's proprietary studies contained erroneous or fabricated data. In the Sensa case, for example, we discovered that the trials included duplicate subjects and that researchers sent weight loss results to the defendants before the test subjects had been weighed. In the Skechers case, subjects who gained weight were reported as having lost weight. That type of fraudulent conduct clearly underscores the need for replication or verification of study results in the orders the FTC seeks against those companies.[11]

With respect to the overall prevalence of weight loss fraud in the U.S. marketplace, the Consumer Sentinel data reflects the types of complaints that consumers are most likely to report to law enforcement authorities. That data does not necessarily provide a representative picture of the prevalence of all forms of consumer fraud. A more accurate and comprehensive picture comes from the FTC's 2011 survey, in which Bureau of Economics staff commissioned a large, nationally representative survey of U.S. consumers on 17 specific categories of fraud. As I noted in my written testimony, that survey revealed that more consumers were victims of fraudulent weight-loss products than of any of the other 16 fraud categories surveyed.

---

[8] *See, e.g., Thompson Med. Co.,* 104 F.T.C. 648, 720–21, 825 (1984), *aff'd,* 791 F.2d 189 (D.C. Cir. 1986); (order requiring well-controlled clinical testing upheld as reasonable fencing-in).

[9] *Telebrands Corp.* v. *FTC,* 457 F.3d, 354, 357 n.5 (4th Cir. 2006).

[10] *See* Hearing Transcript at 73.

[11] *See* Prepared Statement of the Federal Trade Commission (June 17, 2014) at 6–7.

In fact, the estimated number of consumers who were victims of weight loss fraud—5.1 million—was more than double the number of victims in any other category.[12]

Question 7. The FTC's recent enforcement actions, both with respect to weight-loss claims and other health claims, are being closely watched by marketers and advertisers. The Commission now includes as standard language in its consent decrees the requirement that "competent and reliable scientific evidence" consist of "at least two adequate and well-controlled human clinical studies. . .conducted by different researchers, independently of each other, that conform to acceptable designs and protocols and whose results, when considered in light of the entire body of relevant and reliable scientific evidence, are sufficient to substantiate that the representation is true." How are other companies looking at these consent orders supposed to interpret what level of substantiation is now required of them?

Answer. The FTC's use of the two well-controlled study requirement as a remedial matter governing specific types of claims in specific orders does not represent a change in the FTC's substantiation policy and does not necessarily apply to other advertisers. The Commission has made that point clear in the analyses to aid public comment accompanying its administrative consents.[13] Those analyses are published in the Federal Register with links provided in news releases on the FTC website. Moreover, those closely watching FTC's recent enforcement actions will be aware that the agency's orders concerning different types of health claims have variously required two well-controlled studies, one well-controlled study, or more generally, "competent and reliable scientific evidence," depending on the particular claims and products at issue.

In addition, the relevance of specific remedial order provisions to other companies has been the topic of public statements issued by the Commissioners. In the recent GeneLink case, for example, Chairwoman Ramirez and Commissioner Brill, responding to concerns expressed by Commissioner Ohlhausen that advertisers might misinterpret the order's substantiation provisions, clearly stated that "[t]here is nothing in our action today that amounts to the imposition of a "de facto two-RCT standard on health-and disease-related claims." The statement goes on to clarify that the proper level of substantiation is a case-specific factual determination.[14]

Question 7a. Is it reasonable for a company, not yet subject to a consent order, to assume that weight loss or other health claim substantiation that does not include two independent studies will be viewed by the Commission as inadequate?

Answer. Companies looking at the FTC case law and guidance documents, including the Dietary Supplements Advertising Guide, should understand that the Commission's substantiation standard for health-related claims of any kind is intended to be both a rigorous and a flexible standard governed by the specifics of each case. As noted in earlier responses, the Commission evaluates each individual case on its merits, conducting an analysis of Pfizer factors, consulting with experts in the relevant field, and examining the studies upon which a company relies in the context of all of the relevant surrounding literature. In certain situations one high-quality study will suffice to support a claim, in other situations a body of epidemiologic evidence will suffice, and in other situations two or even more studies may be necessary, especially where there are studies with conflicting results. The Dietary Supplement Advertising Guide provides detailed explanations and illustrative examples of the many factors that govern the level of evidence needed to substantiate health-related claims.

Question 7b. How will the Commission ensure that its application of this standard does not have a chilling effect on other firms with regard to otherwise truthful and substantiated claims?

Answer. The Commission ensures that firms understand its flexible but rigorous approach to substantiation of weight loss and other health-related claims by issuing guidance to industry in various forms, providing analysis of its specific orders, and

---

[12] FTC Staff Report, Consumer Fraud in the United States, 2011: The Third FTC Survey (2013), at 17, available at *http://www.ftc.gov/sites/default/files/documents/reports/consumer-fraud-united-states-2011-third-ftc-sruvey/1304lfraudseurvey\0.pdf*

[13] *See, e.g., GeneLink, Inc.; foru Int'l Corp.; Analysis of Proposed Consent Orders to Aid Public Comment,* 79 Fed. Reg. 2662, 2664 (Jan. 15, 2014). The analysis specifically states that the substantiation standard set out in Part I of the order, covering disease claims and requiring two well-controlled human clinical studies, "does not necessarily apply to firms not under order." In fact, that two-study standard does not even apply to all health-related claims made by GeneLink. Part II of the order in that matter sets out a standard of "competent and reliable scientific evidence" for non-disease health benefit, performance, and efficacy claims.

[14] Statement of Chairwoman Edith Ramirez and Commissioner Julie Brill: In the Matter of GeneLink, Inc. and foru Int'l Corp. (Jan. 7, 2014) at 2, available at *http://www.ftc.gov/public-statements/2014/01/statement-chairwoman-edith-ramirez-commissioner-julie-brill.*

engaging in other industry outreach, such as presentations on advertising substantiation at industry meetings. In addition, while the FTC cannot formally evaluate and pre-approve advertising claims, the agency's staff are available to respond to questions and provide general informal advice about the appropriate level of substantiation for claims.

www.ingramcontent.com/pod-product-compliance
Lightning Source LLC
Chambersburg PA
CBHW080830180526
45168CB00006B/2632